The 'Old Guard'
in the
Philippine War

A Combat Chronicle and Roster

Greg Eanes
Colonel, USAF (Ret)

Copyright © 2013 Greg Eanes

All rights reserved.

ISBN 0-9717295-7-3

Previous page photo identified as Private George Tranz, Co. K, Third U.S. Infantry. Photo credits are various and include the U.S. Army Center for Military History, the Library of Congress, the National Archives and Record Administration and Arnaldo Dumindin's *The Philippine-American War, 1899-1902* website (philippineamericanwar.webs.com) and the New York Public Library Digital Library. Photographic materials used consistent with fair use guidelines.

This work satisfies, in part, Virginia Department of Education U.S. History Standard of Learning USII.5a.

Descendants of Spanish-American War veterans (to include the Philippine Insurrection and the Boxer Rebellion) are encouraged to visit the Sons of Spanish-American War Veterans website at www.ssawv.org

DEDICATION

To Private John Franklin Hix,
Company D, Third Infantry Regiment
and his comrades who served during the Philippine War

Lapel Pin of United Spanish War Veterans

and

To the Sons of Spanish-American War Veterans
who keep the 'Spirit of 98' alive

and

To the people of the Philippines with whom we have a special
relationship strengthened by the shared sacrifices of World War II

CONTENTS

	Acknowledgments	i
1	Prelude	Pg 3
2	The Malolos Campaign	Pg 8
3	The San Isidro Campaign	Pg 15
4	Luzon Operations of 1899	Pg 19
5	Luzon Operations of 1900	Pg 50
6	Luzon Operations of 1901	Pg 65
	Appendix 1 Infantry Regiment Composition	Pg 86
	Appendix 2 Campaign Streamers	Pg 88
	Appendix 3 Combat Chronology	Pg 89
	Appendix 4 Regimental Roster	Pg 108

ACKNOWLEDGMENTS

This work has its roots in 1976 when I was a 17-year-old cub reporter for my father's newspaper, The Crewe-Burkeville Journal in Nottoway County, Virginia. I was fortunate as the newspaper offered me opportunities to meet and interview people from all walks of life and I focused on World War II veterans for newspaper feature stories. After seeing one of these, a childhood friend, Larry Echols, remarked that his grandfather, John Franklin Hix, had served in the Spanish-American War. I thought Larry had misspoken and meant World War I or II. He soon produced his grandfather's discharge papers showing service in the Philippine Insurrection and the Malolos Campaign. To my great surprise, Mr. Hix was then still alive at age 102, living in a nearby rest home. Larry and I visited and spent about an hour with his grandfather trying to elicit any recollections he might have about his time in the Philippine Insurrection. While his health was deteriorating, Mr. Hix was still able to recall a few incidents which I eagerly recorded knowing full well that this was likely the only time I'd be able to interview a veteran of the Spanish-American War era. It was a remarkable and memorable moment for me. Nearly 23 years later, working on an American Military University Master's Degree, I took a course on the Spanish-American War. I used the opportunity to write the framework of this study in an effort to learn more about the experiences of John Franklin Hix. That framework led to the work presented here. Thanks to my father Jim R. Eanes for giving me the opportunity to write. Thanks to Larry Echols for telling me about his grandfather. Thanks to the late John Franklin Hix for his service to his country. And not least, thanks to my beautiful wife Rose for her constant support of my writing endeavors.

The Philippine Islands

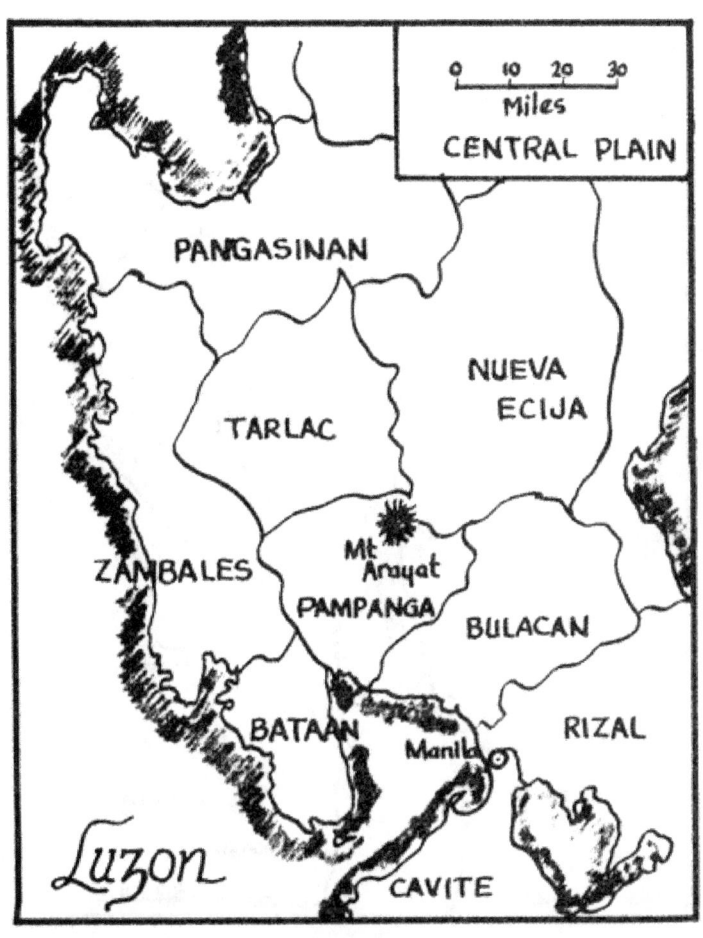

Bulacan and Pampanga Provinces

Area of Operations of Third U.S. Infantry

PURSUIT OF AGUINALDO.

This map of Luzon between the Pampango River and Lingayen Bay shows the position of the several columns of American troops who are said to have surrounded Aguinaldo.

San Francisco Call map showing pursuit of Aguinaldo published on 14 November 1899. The railroad is the Manila to Dagupan Railroad.

CHAPTER 1
PRELUDE

The American presence in the Philippines began with Admiral George Dewey's fleet steaming into Manila Bay. The United States was at war with Spain and the Philippines were a Spanish colony. Dewey defeated the Spanish fleet in Manila Bay on May 1, 1898 but he could not occupy the city because he had no Army. While waiting for that Army, the war with Spain came to an end. As part of the 1898 peace with Spain, that country ceded territories to the United States making it a colonial power with the possession of Guam, the Philippines and Puerto Rico. The U.S. had to assert control over these newly won possessions.

Philippine General Emilio Aguinaldo, a leader in the Filipino independence movement since 1896 had earlier appealed for U.S. assistance in overthrowing the Spanish. For a brief period before the peace with Spain was signed, the Filipino Army and the Americans cooperated in the siege of Manila. Aguinaldo had initially welcomed the American presence. Friction soon developed though when he and other Filipinos realized the Philippines was not going to be granted immediate independence like Cuba. This was complicated by Aguinaldo's claims that Admiral George Dewey's representatives gave official recognition to Philippine Independence movement in talks during the siege of Manila.

These differences did not stop the Filipinos from organizing a government and declaring the First Philippine Republic, "a republican and parliamentary government dominated by an educated elite of intellectuals." The capital city was Malolos in the Luzon province of Bulacan.[1]

Escalating tensions led to a clash between the Philippine Army and

---

[1] Benjamin Beede, editor, The War of 1898 and U.S. Interventions 1898-1934, An Encyclopedia, (New York: Garland Publishing Inc., 1994), 418-419.

U.S. occupation forces outside of Manila on February 4, 1899. This was the initial action in the battle of Manila and America's first Southeast Asian war. It would become known as the Philippine Insurrection[2]. According to historian Michael Clodfelter, "in length, intensity, and casualties [the Philippine Insurrection] deserves to be ranked among the major wars fought by the United States." Among the units serving in that war was the Third Infantry of the United States Army also known as 'The Old Guard'.[3]

Mobilization
John Hix was born on May 22, 1874 in Breckenridge, Ky. He enlisted in the U.S. Army on December 30, 1898 at the age of 24 and assigned to Company D, Third Infantry Regiment of the regular army. Hix said "I enlisted on a warm day in Kentucky. They took us to Louisville the next day and to Chicago the day after that. We arrived in Minnesota in 24 degrees below weather and stayed through January."[4]

The Third Infantry was stationed in the Department of Dakota. Perhaps unknown to Hix, the commanding officer, Colonel John H. Page, had received a mobilization order on December 15 putting the regiment on notice for service in the Philippine Islands.

---

[2] In recent years it has been called the 'Philippine-American War'. For more information see the website of Arnaldo Dumindin, *The Philippine-American War, 1899-1902*. http://philippineamericanwar.webs.com. The best published book on the subject is Brian McAllister Linn's landmark The Philippine War, 1899-1902 (Lawrence, KS: University of Kansas Press, 2000)
[3] Captured documents reveal Aguinaldo was looking for an opportunity to initiate a general uprising as early as January in order to rupture the uneasy peace and capture Manila before the Americans could reinforce in strength. The Americans had likewise developed a campaign plan designed to crush the Philippine Republican Army once hostilities began. See *Adjutant General's Office Official Correspondence*, Captured Documents and New York Times, March 26, 1899, page 3 (hereafter NYT); see also Michael Clodfelter, Warfare and Armed Conflicts: A Statistical Reference to Casualty and Other Figures, 1618-1991, Vol. II, 1900-1901. (Jefferson, NC: McFarland & Company, Inc., Publishers), 418-419.
[4] Personal interview, John Franklin Hix with Greg Eanes, August 1976 and follow-on article, *'Spanish-American War: 102-Year-Old Man Remembers It Well'*, The Crewe-Burkeville Journal, August 26, 1976

According to the order, "It is impossible to state the duration of the tour of service of this character at the present time, but preparations should be made with a view to at least two or three years service before returning to the United States."[5]

Col John Page

Officers and men were allowed full allowance of baggage. Officers and non-commissioned officers were even allowed to take their families. Troops too ill to move or with less than three months service left were to be discharged. The Regiment departed Ft. Snelling by train at 11:45 a.m. on January 30, 1899. Its complement included 24 officers, 1269 enlisted men, one chaplain, three acting assistant surgeons, 15 hospital corpsmen and one signal corps man.[6]

"They took us to Brooklyn, NY then put us on a transport...a ship, the *Sherman* by name..." Hix recalled. "From New York it took us 12 days to get to the straits of the Rock of Gibraltar and the Mediterranean Sea. We went onto the Suez Canal and through the Indian Ocean to the Philippines." The *Sherman* sailed from New York on "early Friday morning" on Feb. 2, 1899 with the Third Infantry Regiment and the second battalion of the 17th Infantry Regiment embarked. They arrived at the Straits of Gibraltar on Feb. 15.[7]

Mr. Hix commented that while on the *Sherman* they ran into a storm. "The officers were on the top deck and the hatchways were

---

[5] **AGO,** *Correspondence Relating to the War With Spain and Conditions Growing Out of the Same including the Insurrection In the Philippine Islands and the China Relief Expedition Between the Adjutant General of the Army and the Military Commanders in the United States, Cuba, Porto Rico, China and the Philippine Islands from April 15, 1898 to July 30, 1902, with an appendix, in two volumes.* **(Washington, D.C.: Government Printing Office, 1902), 854. Hereafter cited as** *Correspondence*

[6] Ibid, 854; Ibid, 865; Ibid, 874; Ibid, 890.

[7] Crewe-Burkeville Journal; *Correspondence*, 893.

covered over. Those high waves looked like they were never going to quit going up and when they started down, they looked like they would never quit coming down," he said.[8]

The Philippines

The *Sherman* arrived in the Philippines on February 28. The Third Infantry Regiment was assigned to the 3rd Brigade of the First Division from March to June 30, 1899. Although Mr. Hix claimed (at the age of 102) to have had "no actual contact" with the Spanish or Philippine guerillas, the back of his discharge papers say he "participated in campaign on and capture of Malolos in March 1899."[9]

Malolos is situated about 25 miles north of Manila on the main road to the interior of Luzon Island. In order to instill control over the Islands, the U.S. Army had to defeat the Philippine insurgents in the outlying areas. The Philippine insurgent force was a significant army. Its estimated strength was between 40,000 to 80,000. Many of them had been effective in fighting a guerilla war with the Spanish and some had formerly served in the Spanish Army in the Philippines. The first nine months of their conflict with the United States was conducted as a conventional war with fixed fortifications and large combat units.

In March of 1899, after the initial clash in which the U.S. Army broke out of the Filipino siege lines around Manila, General Arthur MacArthur, commander of the U.S. Second Division initiated a campaign designed to penetrate central Luzon and destroy the Filipino Army. His main attack was focused on the fortified Filipino defensive line which protected the only railroad in the Philippine Islands.

The Manila to Dagupan Railroad was a British built railway that rain north from Manila into the Pampanga plain coming out at Lingayen Gulf for a distance of about 150 miles. The Pampanga Plain was considered "the breadbasket of the island and strongly

---

[8] Crewe-Burkeville Journal
[9] *Correspondence*; Third Infantry Returns, February 1899; Crewe-Burkeville Journal.

held by the Philippine Republican Army. Thirty to 50 miles wide, the plain was bordered on the east, toward the interior, by the towering ranges of the Beguet Mountains and on the west, near the coast by the Zambales Mountains."[10]

Third Infantry Operations Area

Historian Kenneth Ray Young says, "The best supply line in central Luzon was the railroad, and its capture, with bridges intact and with as much rolling stock as possible, was the major objective of U.S. forces in 1899. To conduct military operations away from its base in Manila, the U.S. Army needed the railroad to transport supplies; the Philippine Republican Army depended on the railroad for supplies from the fertile farming communities located along the 150 miles of track."[11]

---

[10] **Beedee, 460.**
[11] **Ibid**

CHAPTER 2
THE MALOLOS CAMPAIGN

MacArthur's forces captured the railroad maintenance plant at Caloocan five miles north of Manila on March 25, 1899 to initiate the Malolos Campaign. The second battalion of the Third Infantry participated in this attack charging the enemy trenches and serving on the firing line. Companies E, F, G and M were under the command of Capt. S.W. Cook. Companies E, G, and M formed part of the support for the 2nd Oregon Volunteers and ended up joining the second charge on the enemy's trenches. Following this, Companies E and F formed part of the 22nd Infantry's support, were on the firing line by 10 a.m. and engaged until dark. [12]

At Caloocan MacArthur had a command post and armored train built. There were two flat cars and two box cars. The flat cars were mounted with machine guns and a six-pound naval gun. [13]

---

[12] Third Infantry Returns, March 1899.
[13] Tank Net Forum/Blog. Joe Brennan cites an article on the train in "AFV News" Vol 28 No.2 reporting the following info: *"When the armored train was assembled is consisted of 4 cars, 2 box cars in the middle with flatcar at either end. The flatcars were protected by sandbags held in place by the side panels. Only the first flatcar was armed, equipped with a naval 6 [pounder] (57mm) fixed to fire forward, along with 2 Gatling guns on pivots to cover both*

The Third Infantry would concentrate at Caloocan for the next phase of the operation. The remaining battalions of the Third Infantry departed Manila for the front on March 26 at 3:30 p.m. They proceeded by rail to Caloocan and rejoined the second battalion on March 27.[14]

During the next three days the Third Infantry marched from Caloocan through Mycauagan to Guiguinto. On March 30, within one-half mile of MacArthur's headquarters "the regiment came under fire of the advance posts of the enemy." There were no casualties in this action however later that night; a man from Company B was wounded while on guard duty.[15]

Major General Lloyd Wheaton

The campaign plan called for MacArthur's main attack force to advance on the center of the insurgent lines. The Third Infantry, part of Brigadier General Lloyd Wheaton's Third Brigade and Major General H.W. Lawton's First Division, were to press forward in a support move designed to trap an estimated 12,000 armed Philippine insurgents. Another 18,000 Filipinos were said to be in reserve. There were four American brigades involved in the attack.[16]

---

front and sides. ...the disadvantage of the 6 pdr's fixed position lead to addition of a Hotchkiss 37mm revolving gun, capable of firing 60-80 rpm, which could offer further protection to the trains sides...the other 3 cars carried ammunition...and living quarters...Rather than employing a locomotive the train was moved forward by a group of Chinese laborers."
http://208.84.116.223/forums/index.php?showtopic=24238 ,

[14] Beedee, 460; Third Infantry Returns, March 1899.
[15] Third Infantry Returns, March 1899.
[16] Beedee, 460; NYT, March 26, 1899, p.1. Brigades were MacArthur's Division consisting of Gen. Harrison Gray Otis, General Irving Hale,

The American objective was to split the Filipino force in the center, flank them and wheel to the left to crush the divided Filipino army. Wheaton's Brigade was the rearguard of the attack and was to move left and provide a blocking force when the spearhead wheeled left. This would place the Filipinos between Wheaton on the southern flank, MacArthur's advance on the northeast and Manila Bay. These positions would allow MacArthur to take the enemy "in reverse."[17]

It was reported that "under the cover of darkness General Harrison Gray Otis' and General [Irving] Hale's brigades left their trenches and advanced close upon the enemy's line without being detected. Gen. Wheaton's and Gen. [Robert H.] Hall's brigades occupying the vacated positions. At 4 o'clock the American troops breakfasted, and the Filipinos, noticing the camp fires, their buglers called to arms."[18]

The lead brigades advanced to the Filipino lines. The Filipinos held their fire until the Americans were about 1,000 yards away and then let loose a volley, firing low. The Americans returned the volley then charged the trenches "cheering and carrying everything before them". The Americans went straight through the enemy line "cutting the enemy forces in two."[19]

Wheaton's brigade and the Third Infantry remained in the trenches until noon when they were directed to begin the leftward movement. They encountered strong enemy resistance between Malobon and the Tuliahan River but about 4,000 Filipinos or one-third of the Philippine Republican Army was boxed.[20]

Overall U.S. Army commander Major General E.S. Otis reported to Washington that MacArthur struck the center of the insurgent

---

General Robert H. Hall and Wheaton's Brigade of Lawton's Division. The Third Infantry was in Wheaton's Brigade.
[17] NYT, March 26, 1899, p. 1, 3; *Correspondence*, 944.
[18] NYT, Ibid.
[19] Ibid.
[20] Ibid.

line at daylight and was "advancing rapidly and successfully, suffering little." Otis reported the next day, heavy resistance with heavy fighting near Caloocan where the Third Infantry was involved. Otis said they drove the enemy one and one-half miles north across a river.[21]

The first day's fighting resulted in 26 killed and 150 wounded of whom two dead and 12 wounded were Third Infantrymen. Despite the casualties, Otis said the troops were "in excellent condition and spirits."[22]

Malinta Captured
While MacArthur's force drove the enemy, the Third Infantry advanced to place pressure on the Filipinos and was soon faced with insurgents in "strong intrenchments" which had taken months to construct. From these trenches the insurgents offered fierce resistance to the American advance up the railroad to Malinta. A "sharp fight" ensued in which several senior American officers were killed. The insurgent defense, coupled with the terrain allowed the Filipinos to evacuate the town of Malabon which it left burning.[23]

The Filipinos attempted to burn everything of value to include rice mills and bridges. Wheaton's Brigade held the railroad but one of the bridges had been destroyed stalling the Brigade's general advance. Filipinos in fortifications across the Tuliahan River prevented bridge repair work leading Wheaton to direct a pincer movement across the river converging on the rear of the fortifications. The Americans were one-half mile from Malinta.[24]

Wheaton's Brigade crossed the Tuliahan River under enemy fire and pressed on to capture the town of Malinta. According to reports, "When the Americans [were] within about 300 yards of the intrenchments [at Malinta] the Filipinos suddenly volleyed heavily." The Americans captured the town at 1 p.m. MacArthur's

---

[21] *Correspondence*, 944.
[22] Ibid, 945; Congressional Record, *Chronological List of Actions*.
[23] Ibid; NYT, March 27, 1899, p.1.
[24] NYT, March 27, 1899, p.1.

force also pressed its attack and joined Wheaton at Malinta.[25]

Otis reported to Washington, "severe fighting today and our casualties about 40. The insurgents had destroyed bridges, which impeded progress of train and artillery. Our troops met the concentrated insurgent forces on northern line today, commanded by Aguinaldo in person, and drove them with considerable slaughter. They left nearly 100 dead on field, and many prisoners and small arms were captured. The column will press on in the morning."[26]

In reviewing the situation it appeared the entrapment scheme of the U.S. Army failed to meet expectations. Part of this was due to the terrain in which the flanking movements were made but also because of the insurgent army's tactics of contesting every river and stream crossing (which were numerous) and bridgehead from previously selected and fortified sites leading all the way to Malolos. Though in retreat, the Filipino delaying tactics enabled a large number of their troops to escape. This prompted a change of tactics for the U.S. Army which proceeded to press forward and take the Filipino challenges as they met them rather than opting for a single knockout blow through large scale maneuver. The grand prize in the Army's follow-on efforts would be the Philippine Republic capital of Malolos.

Battle for Malolos
On the morning of March 29, MacArthur was only seven miles from Malolos. By 5 p.m. on March 29, he was only three and one-half miles from Malolos. The Filipinos offered "fierce resistance". The insurgent destruction of bridges and railway lines forced the advancing Americans to move the artillery by hand and swim pack mules over contested river crossings.[27]

MacArthur's attack against fortified Malolos began at 7 a.m. on Friday, March 30. It was Good Friday. The Americans drove the insurgents from the beginning. The Third Infantry participated in

---

[25] Ibid.
[26] *Correspondence,* **947.**
[27] *Correspondence,* 950; Ibid, 951.

this final push though most of the fighting involved the state volunteers of MacArthur's brigades. After a 25 minute artillery barrage the men advanced. They succeeded in taking three lines of trenches which were lightly defended.[28]

The Third Infantry formed part of the reserve for the right of the general advance of the line on Malolos. It moved into position "under a thin fire of the enemy and maintained the relative position in reserve during the advance until 10:30 a.m. when the regiment was withdrawn." MacArthur entered the city at 9:30 a.m. after a relatively light battle and less than a week after the start of the campaign.[29]

Aguinaldo apparently realized his position was unwinnable and ordered an evacuation of the Filipino lines during the night. The Filipinos put the city to the torch before leaving. American soldiers helped extinguish the fires after taking the town.[30]

Otis reported the "enemy retired after slight resistance and firing the city." He said a "considerable portion of the city [was] destroyed by fire." The U.S. toll in the final attack was one killed and 15 wounded. Four of the wounded were from Third Infantry. An estimated $1.5 million in enemy supplies were captured at Malolos.[31]

Consolidation

U.S. forces regrouped and attempted to consolidate their lines. Some raiding parties were detailed to active campaigning against suspected insurgent base areas. Other troops were used to provide rear area security in the newly won areas. The American command also used the opportunity to institute a training program for the new influx of regular Army troops replacing the veteran state troops that were destined to go home.[32]

---

[28] *Correspondence,*952; Beedee, 278; NYT, March 31, 1899, p1.
[29] **Third Infantry Returns, Report of Engagements, March 1899; Beedee, 278; NYT, March 31, 1899, p1.**
[30] **NYT, March 31, 1899; Beedee, 278.**
[31] *Correspondence,* **948-949; Ibid, 950;** *Chronological List of Actions*; *Correspondence,* **983.**
[32] **Beedee, 278.**

Otis reported to Washington on April 3, that "present conditions denote insurgent government in perilous condition. Its army defeated, discouraged and shattered; insurgents returning to their homes in cities and villages between here and points north of Malolos, which our reconnoitering parties have reached, and desire protection of Americans. " [33]

The Third Infantry helped chase the scattered insurgents traveling through jungle rivers and lakes outside of Malolos. General Otis advised Washington the enemy army was "much demoralized" by its losses and desertion. He said the Filipino forces "will probably prosecute guerilla warfare, looting and burning [the] country which it occupies." He further reported the middle class Filipinos wanted peace and a stable government but were threatened by the insurgent bands.[34]

Newspaper headlines of the March 1899 offensive.

---

[33] *Correspondence*, 955.
[34] *Correspondence*, 968.

Soldiers of the Philippine Republic

CHAPTER 3
THE SAN ISIDRO CAMPAIGN

Lawton's Expedition
On April 22, Lawton (now north of Manila with 7,000 additional men) led a column of 2500 troops on a six-week long expedition to 'pacify' part of northern Luzon. The Third Infantry, less four companies on railroad guard duty, accompanied Lawton. They were at Norzagary the next afternoon. They were on the way to Calumpit, between Norzagary and Angat, on April 26 when Philippine insurgents engaged Lawton who took light casualties.[35]

The Americans pressed home the pursuit and by April 28 reports were filtering in the insurgent government wanted to suspend hostilities and negotiate an end to the war. This effort collapsed as the U.S. wanted an unconditional surrender before negotiating Philippine independence. On April 29 the Third Infantry engaged the enemy near San Roque in a skirmish lasting about one hour. The enemy was driven from their positions. Three men of the

---

[35] *Correspondence*, 971.

regiment were wounded.[36]

On May 2, the Third Infantry was involved in the capture of Baliuag and succeeded in "scattering" 1600 "strongly intrenched" insurgent troops to the north and northwest. The Americans also captured an estimated 150,000 bushels of rice and 265 tons of sugar.[37]

On the morning of May 4, the Third Infantry was involved in a Division size attack northward to the city of Maasin. According to General Otis, they "crossed [the] river, charged enemy in strong intrenchments, driving him northward and inflicting considerable loss." Lawton moved on to Ildefenso and San Miguel to the north which he captured on May 14 "with slight loss and driving [a] considerable force of enemy."[38]

General Otis reported to Washington on May 17 that "Lawton, with tact and ability, has covered Bulacan Province with his column and driven insurgent troops northward to San Isidro, second insurgent capital, which he captured this morning. Is now driving the enemy northward into mountains. He has constant fighting inflicting heavy losses and suffering few casualties. Appearance of his troops on the flanks of enemy, behind intrenchments thrown up at every strategic point and town, very demoralizing to insurgents and has given them no opportunity to reconcentrate scattered troops."[39]

About 6,000 Filipino forces south of Manila created concern for Otis leading him to order three of Lawton's regiments back to Manila. It was reported "The withdrawal of these troops on May 23 led the insurgents on the northern line to believe that a retreat was intended. They attacked an American column near Baliuag and on May 24 attacked San Fernando. The insurgents were repulsed easily."[40]

---

[36] Third Infantry Returns, April 1899.
[37] *Correspondence*, 981; Ibid, 983.
[38] *Correspondence*, 982; *Correspondence*, 988.
[39] *Correspondence*, 990.
[40] Capt. J.R.M. Taylor's manuscript, <u>History of the Philippine Insurrection</u>,

One of the regiments pulled out of the line was the Third Infantry. The Third, with elements of other units, began a return march south to Malolos around May 22. On May 23, between San Miguel and Baliuag, the American rearguard was repeatedly attacked by a Filipino insurgent force. The rearguard consisted of companies of the Third Infantry Regiment and two companies of the 22nd Infantry Regiment charged with protecting the Signal Corps personnel who were collecting the telegraph wire laid during Lawton's northward thrust.

The troops "left for Baliuag the morning of May 23 and proceeded to San Ildefenso where (the) enemy was encountered and the entire command engaged from 7:45 a.m. to 9:45 a.m. when the enemy were repulsed. The enemy were again encountered at Maasin and engaged for about one hour and driven from their positions. The command proceeded about two miles from Maasin when the enemy made an attack from a strong position, the engagement lasting from 5 p.m. to 7 p.m. when they were defeated."[41]

The second attack occurred about 1:20 p.m. between the village of Maasin and Baliuag. The three battles succeeded in killing two Americans and wounding 13 others. The enemy left at least 16 dead on the field along with a large number of wounded and prisoners. The command arrived at Baliuag about 8:50 p.m.[42]

Press reports of the day's actions say "hard fighting followed from daylight until the Americans camped at night. The troops completed their work, though harassed by the enemy. The troops captured twenty prisoners and thirty rifles. "[43]

The Regiment remained in the Baliuag area guarding trains, performing outpost duty, wagon escort and recon patrols. On May 26, Company C was on a recon four miles from Baliuag on the Satang/San Rafael Road when it was attacked about 6 p.m. by

---

Chapter V, *'The Luzon Campaign'*, 96.
[41] Third Infantry Returns, May 1899
[42] Third Infantry Returns, May 1899; Ibid, Report of Engagement, 1899.
[43] NYT, May 25, 1899.

Filipino insurgents. The company held its position for about two hours when reinforcements arrived and the enemy withdrew. Two Americans were wounded, one dying on June 11.[44]

The *New York Times* reported that on May 24 "General Lawton and most of his troops, has arrived at Malolos. His remarkable expedition marched 120 miles in twenty days, had twenty two fights, captured twenty-eight towns, destroyed 300,000 bushels of rice and lost only six men killed and thirty-one wounded. ...Gen. Lawton estimates that his troops killed 400 insurgents and wounded double that number." This raid ended the spring campaign which had to give way to the monsoon season.[45]

Members of the Third Infantry resting in Bulacan in 1899

---

[44] **Third Infantry Returns, May 1899; Ibid, Report of Engagement, 1899.**
[45] **NYT, May 25, 1899.**

Transporting the Wounded

CHAPTER 4
LUZON OPERATIONS OF 1899

Occupation Force

The Third Infantry remained in place to protect the newly rebuilt railroad which was being used to supply MacArthur's main spearhead. The spring campaign was effectively over in June when the rainy season hit the Philippine Islands. General Otis advised Washington that large segments of Luzon were occupied and that insurgent forces were greatly scattered in bands of 50 to 500. He reported the mass of the people wanted peace and that civil control was being re-established in U.S. occupied areas.

On July 1, President William McKinley recognized the members of the U.S. Eighth Army for their operations in the Philippines and their "willing service through severe campaigns and battles against the insurgents in Luzon, when under the terms of their enlistments they would have been entitled to discharge upon the ratification of the treaty of peace with Spain."

McKinley said "This action on their part was noble and heroic. It will stand forth as an example of the self-sacrifice and public consecration which have ever characterized the American Soldier. In recognition thereof I shall recommend to Congress that a special medal of honor be given to the officers and soldiers of the Eight Army Corps, who performed this great duty voluntarily and enthusiastically for their country."[46]

Reorganization took place on June 30, 1899. The Third Infantry was transferred from Lawton's Division (Wheaton's Brigade) to General MacArthur's Second Division where the Third remained unattached from any brigade. They acted as an independent unit until January 31, 1900. In this capacity the Third acted primarily as an occupation/security force limited to routine outpost duties. This assignment set the pattern for the rest of the war as the 'Old Guard' would, with some exceptions in the Fall 1899 campaign, pretty much remain in Bulacan and Pampangas provinces guarding the Manila to Dagupan railroad, escorting supply trains and conducting daily patrols.[47]

June, July and the first part of August of 1899 were fairly quiet primarily because of the monsoons. The Regiment was in Biltong on August 12 and remained until September 4 when they marched to Pulilan. They operated in the vicinity of Baliung between September 10 and October 30.[48]

The Battle of Bintong Church-August 13-14, 1899

The Battle of Bintong Church began with a simple telegram on a hot Saturday afternoon. On August 12, Captain Arthur Williams of Company B, headquartered in Quingua[49], received a telegram from the regimental adjutant. It was a short message warning him of an insurgent force in that vicinity.

---

[46] *Correspondence*, 1025.
[47] *Correspondence*, Table of Organization, Appendix.
[48] *Correspondence of the Adjutant General's Office Official Records,* (hereafter AGO OR), Microcopy 698, Roll 564, Third Infantry Regiment, Index, Field and Staff, Office Mark 36061.
[49] In 1936, the Quingua's name was changed to Plaridel. It is in Bulacan Province.

Williams decided to investigate the report. He said, "With a small detachment, I proceeded on a reconnaissance up the Bustos road to the parish church, about two miles from here, learned through natives that insurrectos were farther out..." Being late in the day, Williams did not want to be caught without support and returned that evening to his post.

Williams reported his findings and was directed to send out patrols the next morning. Captain William R. Sample (commanding Company D) conducted a patrol south of town towards Guiguinto. First Lt. Arthur M. Edwards (commanding Company B) conducted a patrol of seven men (one corporal and six privates) from Company B towards Bustos.

Edwards' small force moved out about 8:45 a.m. He reported, "I proceeded carefully in scouting formation, being myself very near the front, for about 2 1/3 miles, when I halted my party and went to [a] hedge near by a road to look across the open field with my glasses. In a moment I discovered that there was a line of insurgent soldiers numbering over 50, about 175 yards in advance of us, and advancing toward us. I thereupon turned to have my party return to Quingua to give information, and we were just retracing our steps when a column of insurgent soldiers, numbering about 60, and equipped with rifles and blue and white checked uniform, came into sight around a bend less than 100 yards distant."

Edwards's group was detected and the Filipinos fired on the Americans. Outgunned, outnumbered and enemy closing in from two sides, Edwards sought to find a way out of a bad situation. He said, "Owing to our scarcity in numbers I did not attempt to engage this column, but retreated hastily for about one-half mile, when we were out of sight around a turn in the road. During this first retreat we were fired upon continuously by individual fire...but escaped without any casualties."

Edwards sent two men back to Quingua "with the information I had gained, and I fired several shots at the skirmish line in the field, hoping that they might be heard at Quingua. I then withdrew entirely to meet what re-enforcements that might be sent. These proved to be 25 men of Company B." With the re-enforcements were Acting Assistant Surgeon George S. Pitcher and one acting hospital steward.

Capt. Williams directed Edwards "to take a line covering a road to the ferry crossing." Williams said, "As the men at disposal were very few, the line was very attenuated, and owing to vegetation and the fact that the Bustos road is a continuous village of nipa huts, each surrounded with rough fences of bamboo twigs, it was not found advantageous."

Edwards said his increased force "advanced to the point where I had first seen the enemy and soon discovered him in force and fortified in the Bintong Church and it seemed prudent to withdraw."

Williams used field glasses to watch the Filipinos fortifying the Bintong Church. He observed another 100 insurgents about 800 yards away to his right front "and still others moving to our right and rear." The Americans, now numbering about 33 troops, were facing about 210 Filipinos who appeared to be deploying to capture the small American force.

Williams later reported, "Having located the insurgents and found that they were in force, and my command being very small, I deemed it best to withdraw, as we were in danger of being cut off. In anticipation of that danger I had sent a courier back for reinforcements."

He said, "The enemy did not pursue me, although they did considerable firing." As the Williams-Edwards force fell back, they were joined by Company K under Lt. F.T. Stetson. Company K had been in Quingua while on escort duty from Baliuag and responded to Williams' call for assistance.

Private William Forster was wounded slightly in the right leg just above the ankle about this time. Williams said Forster was hit by a Mauser bullet, "which lodged in [his] ankle...Forster pluckily walked the whole distance back."

Falling back to Quingua, Williams established an outpost with a sandbag breastwork across the Bustos Road to deny access to the ferry across the Bagbag River. He also provided works for interior defense of Quingua to protect against an insurgent attack on his outpost. Williams' total force with B, C and K companies is estimated at about 180 troops.

The location and size of the enemy force was reported to headquarters via telegraph. By 10 p.m. Third Infantry Commanding Officer Col. John Page in Baliuag was directed "to punish this force." Page opted for a classic pincer movement. He directed Capt. L.W. Cooke commanding Companies E, F and G along with Troop K, Fourth Cavalry and one gun of the Third Artillery to proceed from Baliuag on the north side of the Bagbag River, cross it at 4 a.m. and proceed south to Bintong by the Bustos-Quingua Road. Captain Williams with Companies B and D were directed to make a simultaneous northward movement on Bintong from Quingua, also at 4 a.m. Williams' southern force was to serve as the decoy while Cooke's larger force attacked the Filipinos from the northern approaches or the Filipino rear. A blocking action was to support the two attacks with Company I directed to guard the Bagbag River crossing on the shore opposite Bintong.

Cooke's Advance
Cooke recalled, "The morning was very dark, the river had suddenly risen, and one man, Corporal Larson, Company G, was drowned in crossing." The cavalry took the advance and had proceeded three miles from the river crossing when they met and engaged a Filipino outpost on the road. About 25 Filipinos manned the position and opened fire. This initial contact alerted the main Filipino force which deployed to engage the Americans.

Cooke said, "The cavalry dismounted, deployed to the left of the road and began firing volleys" at a range of about 450 yards. The infantry came up with two companies deploying to the left of the cavalry line while the third company remained on the road. The Americans drove the outnumbered Filipinos back taking the outpost but the main Filipino force responded to the scene and began extending its line to outflank the Americans. Cooke said, "The enemy's right overlapped and necessitated a refusal of my left."

It was about this time, Company C appeared as an unexpected reinforcement, dispatched by Col. Page after Cooke's main force had already departed. Cooke said C Company's arrival was "very opportune" as they immediately deployed to refuse the American left flank and protect the main effort.

Cooke's force pressed their advantage in numbers. He said, "The advance was made with great difficulty, owing to the swampy and muddy condition of the rice fields...The engagement lasted for about an hour, my command only halting to fire volleys, when the enemy finally disappeared, passing eastward to my left." Cooke said his men "behaved with great coolness, the officers exercising the most perfect control."

The Southern Force

Williams' southern force started one-half hour late. Williams took all his available men and proceeded north on the Bustos road about 4:30 a.m. "to attract the enemy's attention and give opportunity for [the] force from Baliuag, crossing at Bustos, to attack him."

Company D took the advance with 76 men. Company B was in support. The men packed full canteens and enough food "for a light lunch." Company D's Capt. Sample said, "Half the company was disposed as advance guard, and proceeded cautiously along the Bustos Road toward Bustos. When about two miles from Quingua, fire was heard to our front indicating that a battalion of the regiment from Baliuag, moving to Quingua, had come in contact with the enemy and was engaging him. I hastened the advance as best as the road would permit until sighting scouts of the other battalion, when I moved the company to the right of the Baliuag battalion, which by this time had the insurgents on the run and out of effective range."

By 7:30 a.m. Cooke's force had reassembled on the road and made contact with Williams force. The entire force marched to Quingua.

Williams' men were back in their quarters by 10 a.m. Cooke's force used a ferry to cross the Bagbag River and returned to Baliuag by 5p.m.

Local natives reported 15 Filipino guerillas were killed and an estimated 70 wounded in this action. At least six of the killed were left on the field. Private Charles A. Brooks, Company F was the only American killed in action however two men, Private Max Jackson, Company C and Corporal Peter Larson, Company G, drowned during the crossing of the Bagbag River.

According to native reports the Filipino force engaged was General Pino de Pilar's brigade. The native said Pilar was in direct command of his troops in the engagement and was seriously wounded. According to Cooke, one native "who came in from San Miguel...says General Pilar was there, shot through the body and was spitting blood." Pilar's wounding, coupled with heavy casualties and the concentration of a larger American force undoubtedly influenced the Filipino force to retreat rather than continue operations in the area.

General Pilar

Williams' late departure prevented him from engaging engage the Filipinos. Unfortunately, Cooke's advance came into contact with the Filipinos first, striking their outpost which prevented the main Filipino force from being surprised. Had Williams started on time, he may have engaged first and occupied the Filipino rearguard long enough to enable Cooke's force to surround and block off the Filipino retreat. Cooke said his men "behaved with great coolness, the officers exercising the most perfect control."[50]

---

[50] **Third Infantry Returns, August 1899; Ibid, Report of Engagement. On August 14, 1899, in the vicinity of Bustos, insurgents killed Private Charles A. Brooks, Company F. On August 18, 1899, an insurgent attack near Quingua resulted in a severe leg wound for Private William Foster,**

As a result of Pilar's escape, there would be other engagements between his insurgents and the U.S. Army. Pilar would escape capture each time eventually surviving the conflict by surrendering to U.S. authorities in June of 1900.

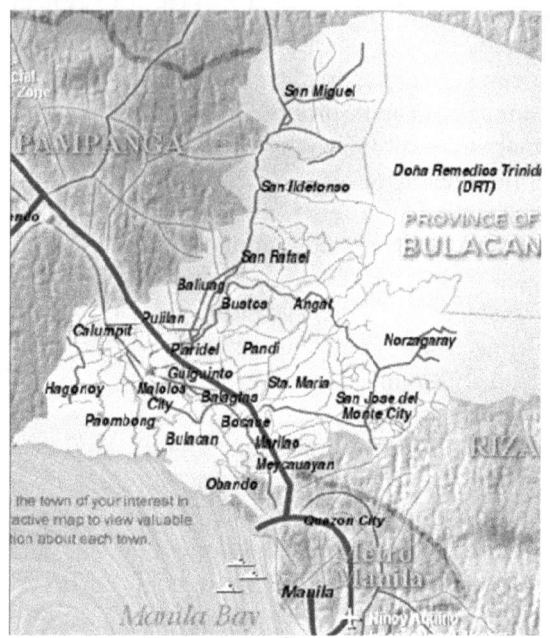

BULACAN PROVINCE[51]

Company B. ; NYT, August 19, 1899, p4.; Brooks was with Company F but NYT reports him as being with Company M; Report of Engagement, Third Infantry, August 13, 1899.; AR 1900, 148-151, After Action Reports of Col. John H. Page, Third Infantry Regiment, August 20, 1899; Capt. Arthur Williams, Commanding Subpost Quingua, August 15, 1899; 1st Lt. Arthur Williams, Commanding Company B, August 15, 1899; Ibid, August 16, 1899; Capt. William R. Sample, Commanding Company D, August 15, 1899; and Capt. L.W. Cooke, commanding Third Infantry Detachment, August 18, 1899.

[51] Map from bulucan.gov.ph, the Province of Bulacan website.

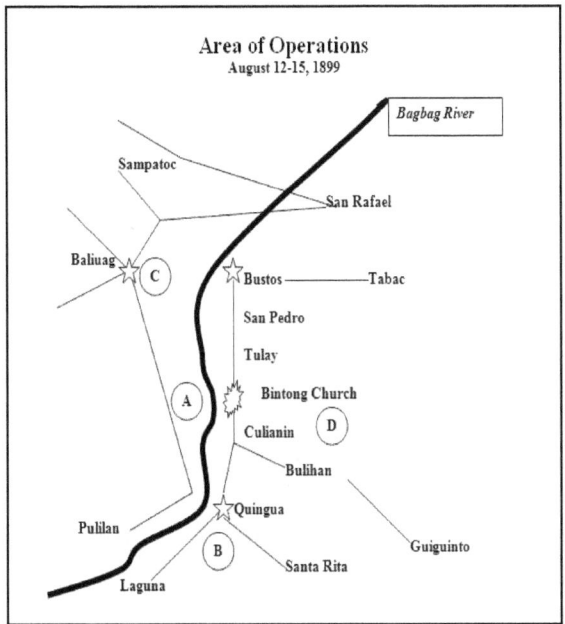

Battle of Bintong Church
August 14, 1899

A. Company I and one 3.2-inch cannon conduct blocking action on Bagbag River crossing across from Bintong Church

B. Companies B and D (about 150 men) depart at 0430 hours for diversionary attack south of Bintong Church. The attack is designed to fix the Filipino force in place so the 2nd Battalion can cross at Bustos and attack from the north.

C. The 2nd Battalion (Companies E, F and G with Co. K, 4th Cavalry) depart at 0400 hours arriving before the southern force and make first contact with Filipino security post. This initial contact eliminates the element of surprise and brings on a general engagement. They are reinforced by C Company as the Filipinos begin flanking the battalion. Total U.S. force engaged: about 280.

D. After approximately one hour, Filipino General Pio de Pilar is wounded. Aware of U.S. forces at Quingua, the Filipinos break contact and escape to the east. Total Filipino force: about 210-250.

More Patrols

This expedition was followed by several recon patrols in September. The two expeditions resulted in some minor gain. One battalion under the command Capt. W.C. Brettler captured 10 prisoners, five rifles and 300 rounds of ammunition on Sept. 6 near San Rafael. A more formidable expedition set off for Pulilan from Baliuag on September 4 in search of an estimated 200 insurgents under General Pilar at that place. Captain L.W. Cooke commanded companies E, F, G and M along with Troop K, Fourth Cavalry and one gun of Light Battery G, Third Artillery.

Cooke said the men "carried rations for one day in their haversacks, 100 rounds of ammunition in their belts, 100 rounds and rations for one day in the wagons, the gun carrying ammunition to the full capacity of its caissons. Axes and shovels were put the wagons incase of mud." They departed at 2:45 a.m. in a heavy tropical downpour that lasted until 10 a.m. The muddy roads forced the column to take the long-way to Pulilan.

Once outside of town the cavalry advanced pushing through to the road to Calumpit. No resistance was met and further inquiries revealed 80 to 200 guerillas under Capt. Ambrosia "had attended a church festival" the previous day. A cavalry squad met about 60 insurgents three miles outside of town but the muddy roads kept the main force from advancing to engage and gave the insurgents time to flee.

Cooke said, "In obedience to the commanding officer's instructions, a careful search was made for rice and other contraband of war. Of rice about 400 bushels was destroyed and 13 head of small cattle was secured." The troops also burned 13 nipa huts known to have been used by guerillas. They returned to Baliuag by 5 p.m.[52]

---

[52] **Third Infantry Returns, September 1899;** *Report of Major General E.S. Otis, U.S. Army, Commanding the Division of the Philippines and Military Governor of the Philippine Islands, Sept. 1, 1899 to May 5, 1899,* **War Department** *Annual Report, 1900,* **Volume I, Part IV, p151-153, afterwards AR 1900; Report of Col. John H. Page, 10 Sept 1899; Report of Capt. L.W. Cooke, 07 Sept 1899; Report of Capt. A. Williams, 06 Sept 1899.**

In addition to the offensive actions by the Third, the Filipino guerillas launched a series of minor harassing actions, firing on various outposts from distances of 800 to 1,000 yard, well out of accurate range. Col. Page reported at least six attacks with no U.S. casualties.

He also reported Baliuag had been cleared of "spies and employees of the enemy" through his use of paid friendly Filipinos. He said the town had been so well cleaned out that "there is an apparent absence of a large number of able-bodied men, who were probably here for no friendly purpose and were an unfavorable quantity in case of trouble." This did not prevent insurgents from keeping track of the Third Infantry's activities however. Page said, "The movements and actions of the enemy in our immediate vicinity have been constantly kept in view. Their system of outposts and detached bodies were well distributed to discover the movements from this post."

The Third sent 19 Filipino prisoners to Manila during the month of September.[53]

Prisoners of War Returned
Near the end of September a Filipino peace delegation from Aguinaldo met American military representatives in an effort to negotiate a peace. This event was met with the exchange of American prisoners of war (though some appear to have been deserters) to include men from the Third U.S. Infantry.

The Associated Press reported the event as follows:

> *Manila, Sept 30 – This has been an eventful day with the northern outpost of Americans at Angeles. Early this morning the Filipino peace commission appeared. The American prisoners followed. Then the commission and*

---

[53] *Report of Major General E.S. Otis, U.S. Army, Commanding the Division of the Philippines and Military Governor of the Philippine Islands, Sept. 1, 1899 to May 5, 1899,* War Department *Annual Report, 1900,* **Volume I, Part IV, p 154, afterwards AR 1900.**

three Spaniards to negotiate for the release of Spanish prisoners, departed up the railroad with a retinue of servants and buffalo carts carrying baggage. At San Fernando the train carrying the commission and prisoners to Manila met a special carrying Major General Otis, Generals Lawton, Bates and Schwan to Angeles on a tour of inspection.

The American prisoners are Corporal Otto Scheu,[54] Privates Albert Rubeck, Otto Wagner and Peter Rollings [Rallings] all of the Third Infantry captured near Baliuag, July 28; Joseph Macideath, James Boyle, William Miller, John Crinshaw, Thomas Dalin, Eli Drew of the Sixteenth Infantry, captured at Caloocan in August; Paul Spillano, Louis Ford, of the Fourth Infantry; Charles Wilander, a discharged Third artilleryman captured by bandits while boating near Malabon; and George Graham, colored, an orderly of the Sixteenth infantry, who was put off the train near Malolos and immediately captured.

At 9 o'clock a group came down the track waving a handkerchief on a bamboo staff and halted before the bridge. A bugle then sounded attention and Major Shields of Gen. Wheaton's staff and five soldiers, with a raised handkerchief, picked their way across the bridge. The Filipinos introduced themselves as Gen. Alejandrius, a slender, bright looking young man of 32, a veteran of the rebellion against Spain; Lieut. Col. Orino and Major Ortes. The latter is of German blood and speaking English fluently.

There soon appeared a second party of fourteen Americans, marching between files of insurgent soldiers. They looked the picture of health and were dressed in

---

[54] **Corporal Scheu is reported in the July 1899 roll as "without leave" with status and location unknown. This is later amplified attesting to his possible capture. Privates Rubeck, Wagner and Rollings or Rallings, are all listed in the August 1899 muster roll as deserters.**

new Filipino uniforms of blue gingham, carrying monkeys and other presents from Filipino friends.

Then Gen. Wheeler, being anxious to see the Filipinos, forded the river, with a correspondent mounted behind. The general's and his staff's horses carry double. General Wheeler shook hands with the Filipinos and there was a general exchange of greetings. The file of barefoot Filipino soldiers curiously surveyed the line of stalwart American sentinels, whose physique contrasted strongly with the little brown men who looked too little for their guns...The prisoners unanimously praised their treatment. One man said: "We have been given the best the country afforded-fine houses for quarters, servants, good food and plenty of wine and money allowance. Aguinaldo visited us and shook hands but three of the boys refused to shake hands with him."

Judging from the stores of the prisoners they have been lionized by the people. They report that five sailors, survivors of Naval Cadet Wood's party, arrived at Tarlac Wednesday. They agree in saying that the Filipinos all say they are "tired of war, but will fight for independence to the last."

The released soldiers also say the idea of independence has taken firm hold of the Filipinos and they threaten, if conquered, to exterminate the Americans by assassination. Aguinaldo, they said, seemed popular among all the people the prisoners met.

The country, they say, is full of rich crops. All the prisoners have stories to tell of interesting experiences. Those captured at Caloocan were marched along the railroads at night through the towns occupied by the Americans...The Filipino commission does not arouse great expectation as to the result of its visit. Major Ortes said frankly they were tired of war, but they decline to say what proposals they bring. The Filipinos lunched with

General Young at San Fernando. Their quarters will be at the Oriente Hotel at Manila.[55]

Another article filed by the *New York Sun* attested to the treatment the Americans received in captivity. It said:

> The American prisoners surrendered to-day say that at first they only received rice as rations. They objected to this, and later on they got coffee, hot rolls, chicken, pork, vegetables and wine. They received an allowance of 20 cents a day for tobacco and luxuries. There was a feast at Tarias on September 17th, and Aguinaldo gave each of the prisoners $4. Each man received $3.50 additional when he reached Mabala Cat. The men were not required to work and were allowed to roam all round the towns. The party started for the American lines on Thursday, but was driven back by the firing of American troops in the attack on Porac.
>
> None of these released American soldiers was captured in battle. The majority of them were taken prisoner while on picket duty at the front or while straying outside the lines. As a matter of fact, several of the men are supposed to be deserters. They say the Filipinos intend to surrender twenty-five more prisoners next Tuesday…One of the surrendered prisoners, a negro of the name of Graham, who was formerly a servant to officers of the Sixteenth Infantry, was commissioned a Lieutenant in the insurgent army and was made much of by the Filipinos. Aguinaldo paid this man's board bill at the Tarlec Hotel, where he was a great pet. The American authorities made a special request for his surrender[56]

---

[55] <u>Oriental American: Official and Authentic Records of the Dealings of the United States with the Natives of Luzon and their Former Rulers</u> by Ora Williams, (Oriental America Publishing Co.: Chicago, 1899), p115-116. This article gained wide circulation in U.S. press.
[56] Reprint; *San Francisco Chronicle*, Sunday, October 1, 1899, p20

Fall Campaign
Effective October 1, 1899, the Adjutant General's Office directed the reorganization and redeployment of the regiment into battalion sized strength for battalion and company level operations. MacArthur's entire Second Division, 16 regiments consisting of 14,000 men and 400 officers, were assigned "the job of repairing, maintaining, and protecting the railroad line from Dagupan to Manila". They established outposts in an estimated 117 towns and villages. The division joined the Third Infantry and shifted from active campaigning to occupation duties. Records suggest elements of the Third Infantry were used as a maneuver strike force.[57]

Due to the reorganization, the First Battalion of the Third Infantry was headquartered in San Fernando. The Third Battalion was headquartered in Baliuag. Companies were posted at various points in the surrounding area. The Second Battalion, under Capt. James McRae appears to have acted as a mobile strike force operating out of San Fernando in support of the First Battalion. This extra strength may have been because the First Battalion was minus Companies B and D which were posted at Guingua. The troops at Guingua "furnished escorts to wagon trains plying between Malolos and Quingua and guards to working parties of natives repairing Quingua-Malolos road. Scouting parties about 10 strong were sent out at least four times a week to reconnoiter roads leading to Bintong and Bustos, to Bulacan and district north of Malolos road." [58]

The repositioning of the Second Battalion caused Colonel Page some anxiety. He reported, "During the first ten days of October and immediately after losing my Second Battalion, large forces of the enemy began to appear in this vicinity (Baliuag)...I deduced that Gen. Pio del Pilar to the north had about 2,000 men distributed along the road from here to Maasim with four field pieces of the gas-pipe type; that General Sario had about 1,000 men to the east and southeast of Bustos; that Colonels Francisco, Ponce and Tecson had about 1,000 men in the vicinity of Pulilan." The

---

[57] **Third Infantry Returns, October 1899; Beede, 279.**
[58] *Otis,* **AR 1900, p154.**

troops were recent levies and more than half unarmed. Page said, "The absence of Second Battalion prevented me from promptly attacking them in detail." Page continued with pacification efforts overseeing the establishment of a civil government for Baliuag on October 30. The town officers consisted of a Mayor and a representative of each barrio.[59]

Among the actions in October 1899 were four combats in Quingua (later Ft. Stotsenberg) where the outposts of Companies B and D were fired on for four successive nights. There were no American casualties reported for these actions. Quingua commander Capt. Arthur Williams said insurgents set fire to nipa huts "in the center of town near [the] church" on the nights of October 7, 8 and 12, 1899. He said the fires took place between 8 and 10 p.m. and were extinguished by the American troops.

On 22 October about 40 men of Capt. Sample's Company D were sent out to rescue two Chinese who were attacked about a mile west of town. They managed to rescue one of the men in an action that resulted in the capture of 12 robbers. They killed one "who refused to halt." This action was followed up the next day when 30 men from Companies B and D with a native scout and a decoy Chinese man "went out toward Dampol, northwest of this post, and captured 10 natives who had assaulted the Chinaman and took a number of bolos." The same night an attack by 25 guerillas was launched on a Company B outpost at Bulacan. According to Williams, "Private Robert McNave, Company B, was shot in the hand during the firing, probably through accidental explosion of cartridge in his rifle."

Two raids on October 25 and 28 resulted in the destruction of insurgent buildings, the capture of 12 prisoners, one Remington rifle and some ammunition. The latter action was an 80 man raid on the village of Lugan, a reported rendezvous for an insurgent company.[60]

There was at least one serious alarm at Baliuag on the night of

---

[59] Ibid
[60] Ibid, 154-155.

October 14/15. The town contained six companies of the Third Infantry, a troop of the 4th Cavalry and two pieces of artillery. There appears to have been an attempt by the guerillas to mount a feint that would tie down force in Baliuag. It was reported, "Outpost[s] on east and north and west flank successively attacked at 9:30, 11:30 and 1:30 last night. No casualties on our side. Careful investigation by scouts and spies allows about 2,000 insurgents and four field guns in the vicinity of Baliuag; 1,200 more are expected when a siege is promised."

This was followed by a report on October 16 suggesting a major effort by the Filipinos. MacArthur reported, "Pio del Pilar has been seen in the vicinity. Total reported to me was about 4,000 but all not being armed...The natives are evacuating all around." Nothing came of the concentration of force however as the insurgents fell back the next day and made a strong demonstration at Angeles where MacArthur's headquarters were located. From Baliuag a 'scout' to Pulilan was conducted on November 7. A total of 11 Filipino prisoners were forwarded to Manila during the month of October.[61]

Capt. McRae was active in the San Fernando region. He led at least two recons in November engaging the enemy on November 9 in Luboa without suffering casualties. A November 24 recon in force to Florida Blanca and Porac resulted in no actions.

Elsewhere though, November 24 proved to be a memorable day. Companies I, K and L with one gun from Battery G, Third Artillery, were involved in two successive combat actions at Maasin and San Ildenfenso. The unit departed camp at 5 a.m. and encountered a small force of the enemy at Maasin. The Filipinos were "routed" after an engagement of about 15 minutes. Later in the day the enemy was driven "out of strong positions" after an engagement of about three hours duration. The latter engagement occurred about 2 p.m. and resulted in the death of Lt. Maxwell

---

[61] **Third Infantry Returns, October, 1899; AGO OR, Index, F&S, Office Mark 36061; AR 1900, 217; Ibid, 218; Ibid, 242. All outposts were connected by telegraph line; Ibid, 154.**

Keyes who was shot and killed instantly "while leading scouts."⁶²

An important theatre action took place in November while the Third Infantry conducted its rear area patrols. On November 29, after a 12-day march of 60 miles with a handpicked force of 1,000 men, MacArthur succeeded in reaching and capturing Dagupan, the end of the rail line from Manila, from the insurgent forces. This action was part of a larger offensive involving three major U.S. forces in north Luzon and effectively ended the war of movement phase of the insurrection. At this time, "All regular and systematic tactical operations ceased."⁶³

Otis reported to Washington on December 7:

> "*In central Luzon no insurgent force of importance except in Bulacan province, near mountains, where [Gen. Gregorio Del] Pilar holds together 1,000 or more men, which will be attacked soon...Many small insurgent armed bands in country robbing, and in some instances murdering, inhabitants, which are being pursued by troops quite successfully.*"⁶⁴

Otis said nearly all enemy artillery, supplies, rifles and ammunition had been captured. He said "Aguinaldo's army, which had formerly occupied the line of the Manila and Dagupan railway and which still retained organization was being pressed continuously by General MacArthur" into the Zambales and Bataan mountains. He felt MacArthur's troops would defeat the insurgent remnants.⁶⁵

December for the Third Infantry involved routine patrols spiced up by action on two raids. Companies A, B, and C joined a detachment of the 16th Infantry on a four day expedition from Baliuag. They engaged the enemy near San Ildefenso on Dec. 4 and Maasin on December 6, suffering no casualties. On December

---

⁶² **Third Infantry Returns, November, 1899; AGO OR, Index Office Mark 36061;** *Correspondence***, 1109, Otis to AGO, dtd November 27, 1899; Third Infantry Returns, November 1899; Ibid, Report of Engagement.**
⁶³ **Beedee, 279.**
⁶⁴ *Correspondence*, **1115.**
⁶⁵ *Otis*, **AR 1900, p310.**

10, the enemy was again struck near San Ildefenso without casualties to the Americans.[66]

Grant's Expedition (4 to 21 December 1899)[67]

Capt. McRae remained busy with Companies E, F, G, and H selected to serve in Brigadier General Frederick Dent Grant's expedition into southwestern Pampanga, Bataan and Zambales to clear it of insurgents.

Grant commanded an area designated as the Fifth District. It consisted of the Provinces of Bataan, Pampanga and Bulacan on the Island of Luzon.[68] The 49-year-old general was the oldest son of former President and General of the Army Ulysses S. Grant. At the age of 11, he accompanied his father's regiment when it marched into northern Missouri when the Civil War erupted. Later sent home, he would visit his father during several campaigns. He went to West Point in 1866, graduated in 1871 and had a variety of assignments to include serving with George Custer on the Black Hills Expedition. He was in the 1878 Bannock Indian War eventually resigning from the Army in 1881 serving by 1889 as U.S. Minister to Austria-Hungary. He returned to active duty in the Spanish American War, promoted to Brigadier General of Volunteers and served in Puerto

BG Frederick Dent Grant

---

[66] **Third Infantry Returns, December 1899.**
[67] *Annual Report of the War Department, for FY1900*, **Part 5. Details contained in the *Report of Operations of Second Brigade, Second Division Eighth Army Corps, from November 1, 1899 to April 15, 1900 by Brig. Gen. F.D. Grant, U.S.V., Commanding* (15 April 1900) and appendices and McRae's Report to AG, Second Bde, Second Div, Eighth Army Corps, dated 10 January 1900 in *Annual Report*, Part 6, page 366.**
[68] *Annual Report of Brigadier General Arthur MacArthur*, **Exhibit C, Roster of Troops Serving in the Division of the Philippines, July 15, 1900.**

Rico. Sent to the Philippines, he was made Brigadier General in the Regular Army.[69] His Fifth District command initially consisted of two troops of the Fourth Cavalry, Light Battery E of the First Artillery, the Third, 32nd and 35th Infantry Regiments, six companies of the 22nd Infantry and 10 companies of the 41st Infantry. This basic force structure might shrink or swell depending on theater wide mission requirements. Many of the troops were detached as security in village outposts.

Grant's 750-man force would maneuver from Dinalupijan (in the south), through Balanga (the provincial capital of Bataan) over the mountains to Subic Bay to unite with an American column attacking from the north (along the coast) and a Naval and Marine landing force at Subic. Grant's southern force consisted of 400 men of the 32nd Infantry, 300 men of the Third Infantry and 50 men or one platoon (two guns) of Battery K.[70] The northern force was the 25th Infantry (400 men) from Bamban. The 25th Infantry would pass through Iba, the capital of Zambales.

The columns were supported by local native or Chinese "burden bearers" or "litter bearers",[71] ponies, bull carts and wagons. All men were dismounted so horses[72] could be used to help transport

---

[69] Grant died of cancer in 1912 with the rank of Major General and is buried in the cemetery of the U.S. Military Academy at West Point.

[70] The 32nd was commanded by Colonel L.A. Craig; Battery K was commanded by Captain C.W. Hobbs. Other Third Infantry Officers (and assigned duties) included 1Lt. James T. Moore, Adjutant; 2Lt Oliver H. Dockery, Jr., Quartermaster and Commissary, 1Lt George E. Houle, commanding Company H; 1Lt C.B. Humphrey, commanding Company G, Topographical Officer and 1Lt Frank S. Burr, 11th Inf, attached to the Third Inf and commanding Company F; 2Lt Walter E. Stewart, commanding Company E.

[71] Four litter bearers per company were normally allowed and could reportedly carry up to 50 pounds of supplies. Noted in General MacArthur's Annual Report, "During action, these men were of great use in carrying off the dead and wounded and in bringing up ammunition, and considering their class and small pay, showed considerable courage in their work." Most of these were discharged when active operations ceased and occupation became the norm. Appendix D, page 4 of the 1 October 1900 report. See also Grant's report of the operation.

[72] The infantry's use of horses became common in the Philippines due to the terrain and nature of the counterinsurgency mission requiring sustained

rations and ammunition. Besides the ammunition carried on their belts, a reserve supply of 100 rounds per man was carried in the trains while another 50,000 rounds were carried in the wagons with 7,000 rations, cooking utensils and baggage. Each man was to have a blue flannel shirt and at least one blanket for every two men. The Khaki blouse, poncho and shelter tent were optional though each company had to carry at least two axes and two spades. Navy gunships were to meet them on the coast to resupply and also to cooperate in combat actions.

Grant directed native bearers paid weekly "in order to attach them to the United States Government by a sense of self-interest". He reported, "It was specially enjoined on the command that everything taken from the natives should be paid for promptly, with a view to aiding the pacification of the country, and strict orders were issued against looting, and against offending or intimidating the natives, and especially against interfering with women."[73] He forbid entering a private dwelling "except in active pursuit of an enemy, or unless he is a member of a party ordered to search for arms and ammunition, or is quartered there, or has business therein upon which he has been ordered by competent authority". He also directed appointment of a provost officer "among whose first duties will be to search the town and destroy 'vino'" noting that "Commanding officers will be held personally responsible for the conduct of their men, and any damage done by them will be assessed under the provisions of the fifty-fourth Article of War."[74]

---

patrols, scouts over large areas, and rapid movements over difficult terrain, often made worse in the rainy season. They became 'mounted infantry'. One quartermaster reported, "The escort service finally reached such proportions, and entailed so much travel on foot troops that in order to meet such demands, an issue of fifty horses was made to each regiment of infantry." See MacArthur's *Annual Report* for 1 Oct 1900, *Gen. Wheaton's Report*, p42, Exhibit C, *Report of the Office of the Chief Quartermaster*, Department of Northern Luzon, Major Robert R. Stevens.

[73] Ibid, p69. The Northern column consisted of 17 officers, 400 enlisted men, a pack train of 20 ponies and a detachment of 100 native bearers carrying ammunition and rations. It was under the command of Captain J.P. O'Neil.

[74] Ibid, Appendix D, p98

McRae's Battalion

Capt. McRae selected 75 men each from companies E, F, G and H for 300 enlisted men.[75] Attached were three "hospital-corps" men, 16 Macabebe litter bearers and 20 native burden bearers. They concentrated at Guagua and marched at 8:30 a.m. for Dinalupijan "upon which place a combined attack was to be made at daylight on the 4th by a battalion of the Thirty-second Volunteer Infantry from Florida Blanca" and by McRae's battalion. A bull-cart train of supplies was added at Lubao before continuing in the afternoon.

McRae marched during the night of 3 December. He found bridges at stream crossings destroyed causing the unit great difficulty in crossing. A major river crossing occurred at the Almasenes River at 9:30 p.m., a distance of about 150 yards.

Though pitch black, Sgt. William H. Deavey, Co. H, "without a moment's hesitation, plunged into the Almacenes River...the night being dark and the water deep, and with the assistance of others managed, after much hard work, to get a large raft into a position which enabled the rest of the command to cross."[76] He was ably assisted by Lt. George Houle and a few others, swimming across to obtain small boats and rafts.

The crossing was completed by 11:30 p.m. McRae reported:

> "While the advance was crossing the river signals by the enemy (calls and by fire) were observed in the small village opposite to where we crossed. Signals were seen from the time we left Lubao—columns of smoke during the day and fires at night. The advance guard moved forward, as soon as it had crossed the river, through the village, which in the meantime had been deserted, and

---

[75] Third Infantry Officers included McRae, 1st Lt James T. Moore, Adjutant, 2nd Lt Oliver H. Dockery, Jr., quartermaster and commissary, 1st Lt C.B. Humphrey, commanding Company G and topographical officer, 1st Lt Frank S. Burr, 11th Infantry (detached to Third) commanding Company F, 2nd Lt Walter E. Stewart, commanding Company E and Acting Assistant Surgeon Francis McCallum.

[76] Deavey was awarded a Certificate of Merit for his "gallant conduct" here. See AGO General Orders (GO#107), July 1, 1905.

> came to and entered Llana Hermosa without opposition about 11 p.m. This place was almost entirely deserted when the advance guard arrived. A bull cart containing 24 Filipino flags and about 800 rounds of ammunition, which was attempting to escape, was captured by the advance guard."[77]

The remainder of McRae's force arrived by 12:30 a.m. resting in the town square. They dried their clothes over fires from about 1 to 3:30 a.m. (4 December). The Americans found the Filipino telegraph wire and cut it at 1 a.m.

McRae arrived at Dinalupijan at 5:30 a.m. or "just as day was breaking" on 4 December. They had marched 25 miles at night. McRae reported:

> "When about three-fourths of a mile of Dinalupijan the advance was fired upon by the enemy's outpost. The outpost was driven in. A company was then deployed to the right of the town and another to the left and the town entered from the south. After a slight resistance the enemy fled toward the north, mixing with the fleeing refugees. Three insurgents, one a captain, were killed and buried by our troops, and probably a number of others were killed and wounded who did not fall into our hands, and 9 prisoners, 7 rifles, and a number of bolos were captured. There were about 200 insurgents in town at the time of our arrival. After chasing the fleeing insurgents 2 or 3 miles, recall was sounded and the troops assembled on the plaza, outposts having been established." [78]

The 32nd Infantry and two guns from Battery K arrived at 6:30 a.m. too late for battle. General Grant gave the Third Infantry the advance on 5 December and the expedition departed at 9:00 a.m.

---

[77] McRae's After Action Report, No. 121, AR Part 6, p367.
[78] Ibid; see also Grant's report, Grant reported, "Three dead bodies were found with guns in their hands, and seven other rifles were secured...".

In a "slight skirmish" at Orani the morning of December 5, McRae again drove a force of the enemy killing two, taking four prisoners and capturing two revolvers and six homemade cannon. The battalion remained overnight in Samal and transferred extra rations from the bull carts to the burden bearers. They departed at 6 a.m. on 6 December entering Balanga about 8:10 a.m. McRae's force was fired on but there was no significant opposition. They captured two insurgents trying to destroy a bridge, and a rifle, a carbine, a revolver and one saber. Grant arrived at 11 a.m. and the town was occupied until 4 p.m. when the entire American force fell back to Dinalupijan for the next phase. Grant reported, "The enemy were evidently fleeing before our troops in all directions, not caring to risk an engagement."[79]

To facilitate the movement to Subic, Grant regrouped and trimmed his force. Lt. Burr took 200 men of the Third Infantry and the sick and left the expedition. Third Infantry Companies F and G, 25 men each from Companies E and H and the supply train were directed to Florida Blanca and a return to their normal posts.[80] The terrain also made it impractical for artillery so it was sent back on 8 December. This left only 100 men[81], hand-picked by McRae for their good physical conditions, and the 32nd Infantry to complete the expedition. They would have to climb a mountain to get to Olongapo and Subic. With three days rations and 160 rounds of ammunition, the force departed at 4:30 a.m. on 9 December.

Grant sent the force over in group intervals. Ninety men of the 32nd Infantry made up the first element to travel over the mountains. It was felt the smaller groups would invite attack and allow an engagement. Three columns, to include McRae's, met on the summit. Grant reported, "It is worthy of note that the detachment of Capt McRae marched the whole distance over the mountains in the one day." The U.S. force seized Olongapo by 5:30 p.m. on

---

[79] Ibid, p71.
[80] The expedition had stripped this manpower from rear area security duties. The minimal opposition, the need for rapid movement and the need for these men at their posts likely caused their early return.
[81] Lt. Houle, Commanding Co. H and Lt. Stewart, Commanding Company E. Also with McRae were Acting Assistant Surgeon McCallum, 1 hospital-corps man, the Macabebe litter bears and native burden bearers.

December 9 after a 20 mile march over a mountain. McRae says it was without opposition but the 32nd faced was engaged as Grant reports killing two insurgents, wounding two, capturing six stores. McRae said, "The Spanish naval arsenal fell into our hands" and included an extensive inventory of captured equipment used to repair ships and weapons.

The Navy arrived on the morning of the 10th to find the Army in place. The Marines took control of the Olongapo and Grant's expedition boarded the ships for a seaborne assault on Subic.

On December 10, McRae's 100 men[82] with the 32nd Infantry landed at Subic and drove the enemy killing two insurgents and capturing two rifles, 200 rounds of ammunition, 1200 bushels of rice and 300 pounds of salt, foodstuffs for the insurgents. The combined force marched on December 11th to unite with the 25th Infantry at San Marcelino on the 12th. Returning to Subic they engage insurgents killing two while simultaneously rescuing about 25 Filipino and Spanish prisoners from captivity. They returned to Subic that day.

Capt James McRae - 1892 Photo

On 13 December, McRae's detachment was scouting near Olongapo and engaged insurgents killing one. They destroyed a blockhouse formerly used as an insurgent signal station. Later that day they kill one and wound two insurgents while capturing two carabaos, two ponies and a cartload of insurgent clothing. On 15 December, marching into the village of Marcelino, they discover

---

[82] **The Third Infantry was embarked on the gunboat *Mindoro*.**

and release an Englishman who had been held prisoner by the insurgents. Elements of McRae's force also participate in the 16 December capture of the insurgent steamer *Don Francisco*.

The 32nd and McRae's force (less a 13-man horse detachment under Lt. Humphrey traveling overland to Guagua the day before) embarked on the quartermaster boat *Mactan* at 9:30 p.m. for a seaborne night attack on Mariveles. At 2:30 a.m. they land on each side of town and surround it before daylight. The town was entered at first light on 18 December. One insurgent is wounded, one is killed and two are captured with three rifles. The force returned to the ships at 6:30 a.m. and proceeded to Manila returning to their primary outposts at Santa Rita and Bacolor on 20 December.

McRae reported the total distanced marched at approximately 165 miles, total distance by steamer was about 90 miles and distance by rail about 38 miles. In his report, McRae noted:

> *"excellent work done by First Lieut. James T. Moore, battalion adjutant, Third Infantry, who, while in command of the mounted scouts of the detachment, led the advance into Orani, Samal, Abucay and Balanga on the 5th and 6th of December, and by his good judgment and intrepid conduct adding greatly to the celerity and success of our movements, and by First Lieut. George E. Houle, Third Infantry, at the crossing, in the face of the enemy, of the Almasenes River near Llana Hermosa on the night of December 3. Lieutenant Houle was in command of the advance guard, and with a few selected men swam to the opposite shore at peril to his life, and with excellent and great energy bridged over the deepest portion of the river by means of rafts, over which the command crossed."*[83]

General Grant reported:

> *"One of the results of this expedition, besides the very considerable number of arms and property captured, of*

---
[83] **McRae's After-Action Report, p368**

the enemy killed and wounded, and of Spanish and American prisoners released, was the demonstration to the native population that the American soldier need not be feared by those having peaceful intentions. Very shortly after the occupation of the towns by our troops the population, which had run away in terror at our approach, returned to resume their avocations. Small parties of the enemy have continued to rob and in some instances murder the natives, as well as to attack small detachments of our troops by ambushing them. Many thousand natives who have desired to discontinue any participation in the insurrection have been enabled to do so by the presence of our troops, and a very large quantity of insurgent property has been destroyed in this territory."

Grant praised the detachment officers stating they "conducted the work committed to their charge with skill and judgment."[84]

Aguinaldo Changes Strategy

Two combat actions also occurred on December 11 when Companies A, B and C engaged the enemy twice near San Miguel and San Ildenfenso. After that, the regiment concentrated at Quingua for deployment to Caloocan where it was reorganized for security operations. The Third's primary responsibility shifted from a maneuver force to a security force with orders on December 13 to "replace the 16th [Infantry] on [the] railroad" so the 16th could be used for operations "elsewhere."

December also saw a change in Aguinaldo's war strategy. He succeeded in escaping the last American offensive. Realizing he could not win, Aguinaldo directed his army disperse to their native provinces and conduct guerilla operations. In this the Filipinos were successful though Aguinaldo lost much of the control and coordination he had before the guerilla phase. Independent guerila units attacked "garrison towns, set booby traps, and attacked patrol parties repairing the railroad and telegraph lines."

---

[84] Ibid, p76

They also conducted ambush operations and harassed supply lines. They were supported by the general population, sometimes through coercion. The guerilla attacks were designed to tire the Americans and influence the on-going American political debate over the fate of Philippine islands.[85]

Macabebe Scout Operations

One of the Third's first operations from Caloocan involved an expedition with Philippine Scouts. First Lieutenant J.T. Moore, Adjutant of the Third Battalion, commanded a detachment of 125 Macabebe Scouts on a boat expedition from December 28 to January 1, 1900. Moore's mission was charged with scouting the area around Paombond and the area south and west of Bulacan and extend Army operations as far east as Obando.

Moore reported the raid left Caloocan in boats (bancas) at 1 a.m. on December 28

Macabebe Scouts

reaching the outskirts of Paombong in time to surround and enter the town at daylight. There was no indication of insurgent activity. Reembarking in the boats, the force proceeded to Bulacan with a part of the force scouting the road between Atlog and Bulacan

Moore said, "The bancas had to be pulled and pushed by hand over a mile before reaching Atlong on account of the low tide." The

---

[85] Ibid; Congressional Record, *Lists of Engagements*; AR 1900, 304, Lawton to Schwan, 12/11/99, "the Third Infantry will take line of railroad from Caloocan to Calumpit" and relieve 16th Infantry; Beedee, 279.

force reached Bulacan about 5 p.m. The next day the force split again scouting the area. Moore's force reached Obando about 8p.m. The second force ran into a party of five bandits, taking one prisoner along with a rifle and two swords dropped in flight.

Both parties returned to Bulacan on the 30th and proceeded back to Caloocan on December 31 arriving about 3 p.m. on January 1. Moore reported, "There was no evidence of any armed insurgents in the country traversed, and it is my belief that no such party exists." He said, "In the small villages visited the people seemed hard at work fishing, cutting nipa, and collecting the nipa sap."

He reported, "We were greatly handicapped by the lack of water in the streams at low tide, making progress slow." He said, "Bancas that have to be poled are of no use on a scout of this kind, those that carry four or five men and propelled by paddles being the only one practicable." He said, "About three-quarters of a mile from the bay, in each of the rivers Santa Cruz and Pamaranan, are barriers of spikes and rocks, probably constructed in the time of the Spanish insurrection to prevent gunboats from ascending the rivers."

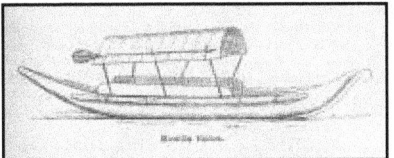

Banca Boat

One unusual incident occurred while the force was in Bulacan. Moore reported at about 7 a.m. in broad daylight, a Macabebe scout disappeared "and it is supposed he was killed; no trace of him could be found, although several search parties were sent out."[86]

---

[86] Ibid; Congressional Record, *Lists of Engagements*; AR 1900, 304, Lawton to Schwan, 12/11/99, "the Third Infantry will take line of railroad from Caloocan to Calumpit" and relieve 16th Infantry.; AR 1900, p305, Chief of Staff Theodore Schwan to General Arthur MacArthur, Dec. 13, 1899. MacArthur replied the same day, "A large part of the battalion of the Third Infantry now stationed at Guagua, Bacolor and Santa Rita is with General Grant in the mountains of Bataan and Zambales, and cannot be very well reached for a week or ten days." Report of 1st Lt. J.T. Moore, January 2, 1900. The prisoner was turned over to the commanding officer at Malolos.

While nothing was found on the expedition, Major Johnathan W. Hannay, Commanding Third Battalion, said, "Lt. Moore has performed a novel and arduous duty with credit." The experience gained may have led to a change in the conduct of such banca patrols when the rivers were low and less conducive to navigation. Major Hannay observed that larger bancas "would be useful as supply depots or assembling points from which the smaller bancas could operate."

A second expedition was launched within the week and with greater success as the Macabebe Scouts located an insurgent barracks on an isolated island. First Lt. Tenney Ross and 2nd Lt. O.H. Dockery, Jr. led an expedition of 71 Macabebe scouts about 1 a.m. on January 8 and proceeded towards Malolos where a "company of insurgents was reported to have its headquarters."

After getting lost in the nipa swamps, the expedition eventually reached Pamorong where a local was persuaded to lead the expedition to the hiding place of the insurgents. Ross reported, "The detachment reached Taurran, which is located upon a small island in the swamps about one mile from Atlog, at about 12 o'clock noon, and was fired upon by about 40 insurgents. The scouts returned the fire and charged the enemy, who immediately gave way and scattered in the swamps, some going in the direction of Atlong and Malolos."

Tenney said, "Taurran had evidently been a rendezvous for the insurgents for some time, and here was discovered a cuartel [barracks] well provided with armra[c]k[s] and other conveniences. Near the cuartel were ten or a dozen buildings, which I learned were used by the officers and families of the insurgents. In one of these shacks, Lt. Dockery found and destroyed over 1,000 rounds of Remington ammunition, but although all the other buildings were most thoroughly searched, nothing else of importance was found. I burned the cuartel and every other building on the island." The detachment was back in Malolos by 3 p.m. and returned to Calumpit the next day.[87]

---

[87] **Report of First Lieutenant Tenney Ross, January 9, 1900**

KILLED IN ACTION - General H.W. Lawton, under whom the Third Infantry served for a time, was killed in action in the Philippines in 1899. This is one of the last photos taken of Lawton before his untimely death by sniper during the battle of Paye. He was the only general officer killed in the Philippine-American war and a Civil War recipient of the Medal of Honor when a Captain in Company A, 30th Indiana Infantry during the battle of Atlanta.

CHAPTER 5
LUZON OPERATIONS OF 1900

Outpost of Company D, Third U.S. Infantry at Quingua, Bulacan

To establish security in the countryside U.S. Army units were detached into company level detachments and assigned permanent stations at key population centers. Otis said, "The character of the service which our troops were called upon to perform in Central Luzon from the time they occupied the entire railway country to February is indicated...They were widely scattered in detachment, company and battalion organizations, guarding centers of population and points deemed important for strategic purposes and concentration."

The Third Infantry was eventually concentrated at Manila for redeployment to outposts. The transport *Mactan* transported a portion of the regiment from the field to Manila and the entire army was reorganized in February 1900 "so as to furnish the best protection possible to the inhabitants, and at the same time reunite regimental organizations within the same sphere of action."[88]

An analysis of message traffic and monthly returns affecting the Third Infantry indicates their stations serviced smaller 20-man detachments in adjacent barrio or village outposts. The Third

---

[88] *Otis*, AR 1900, 347; Ibid, 337; Ibid, 422

Infantry outposts appear to have been situated within eight to 12 miles from each other. The smaller outposts may have been rotated to and from the company headquarters area.[89]

Daily patrols consisted of about six men and were routinely led by a corporal or sergeant. Periodically, platoon size elements (35-50 men), led by a company grade officer would conduct 'scouts' in the outlying parts of the company area of operation (AO). These 'scouts' were large patrols that maintained contact with existing outposts, collected intelligence and acted as a strike force for targets in their AO.

While assigned the primary responsibility of guarding and protecting a segment of the Manila to Dagupan railroad, the Third Infantry also provided security and escorted wagon trains on the Manila-San Fernando Road which ran parallel the rail line. The Third Infantry's Headquarters element was initially stationed at Caloocan outside of Manila with outposts placed in Pampanga Province and Bulacan Province.

By April 1900, the Headquarters would be moved northward to San Fernando with the southernmost outpost being Meycauayan. The various outposts also commanded key lines of communication into the central plains north of Manila. The plains are home to the major roads and Pampanga River which has a series of smaller tributaries and swamp lands. The rivers and swamps were patrolled by Army troops using native Filipino boats called bancas.

McRae's Expeditions

The year began as it ended with the first and third battalions at their respective stations along the railroad patrolling and scouting the area in small detachments. They entered the 20th Century without incident however an unidentified Third Infantry detachment did engage insurgents on January 2, 1900 near the village of Florida Blanca.[90]

---

[89] Taylor, History, 13HS, Chapter VI, *'The Period of Guerrilla Warfare, Nov. 13, 1899 to July 4, 1902'*.
[90] Congressional Record, *List of Engagements*.

The next day Capt. James H. McRae led a scouting detachment consisting of troops from Companies F and G from San Jose to the village of San Pedro 12 miles away. In a brief action the unit captured 24 rifles and 1000 rounds of small arms ammunition.[91]

This action may have whetted McRae's appetite for more. On January 7 he departed San Jose with Companies F and G "for the purpose of cleaning up the adjacent country and clearing it of insurgents." A series of combats followed. On January 9 the expedition hit Quila; Pulanlay on January 11 and Florida Blanca on January 12 all of which resulted in the capture of rifles, ammunition and insurgents.[92]

The 'Moveable Column'

During the period of 12 January to 6 February 1900, McRae led a 'movable column' consisting of Companies F, G and 50 Macabebe scouts.[93] This mobile strike force was broken down as follows:

Captain James H. McRae – Commanding
- 1st Lt James T. Moore, Commanding Macabebe Scouts
- 1st Lt John W. Barker, Commanding Company F
- 1st Lt C.B. Humphrey, Commanding Company G[94]
- 1st Lt Frank S. Barr[95], Commanding a Co. G mounted detachment (32 men) and 15 Macabebe Scouts
- Acting Assistant Surgeon Francis McCallum

---

[91] Third Infantry Returns, December 1899.
[92] Ibid.
[93] *Annual Report*, Part 6, p369, McRae's Report to Adjutant General, 2nd Brigade, 2nd Division, No. 122, 23 Feb 1900.
[94] 2nd Lt Robert I Rees was also on duty with Company G; Humphrey was also serving as the Quartermaster and Topographical Officer.
[95] Lt Barr was of the 11th Infantry but was attached to Company G.

This expedition, in two columns and different routes, started on the morning of 12 January passing through several towns before uniting at San Pablo Grande at 9:30 pm about 18 miles from their start point. McRae reported the houses were searched at each location the "natives lined up on the plaza for investigation." Only one Mauser rifle was discovered in Barurya but one insurgent officer and 25 soldiers were identified by Spanish guide "who had recently been captured as an insurgent first sergeant, and therefore knew the insurgents personally." Some scouts were also fired on and returned fire but the insurgents escaped in the woods.

The combined command departed at 6 a.m. on 13 January marching to the Lampac Mountain. McRae said, "This almost inaccessible insurgent stronghold was found deserted. A hospital building and barracks for about 500 were burned. One small brass cannon was found on the mountain." They traveled through several more villages before arriving at San Jose, Florida Blanca without incident. They traveled to Porac the next day without incident. McRae noted his effective strength at six officers, 145 enlisted men and 45 Macabebe scouts.

On 15 January the column reached Banaba capturing a prisoner and liberated a Spanish prisoner. Another Spaniard was liberated and three more prisoners taken near Palusapis. A debriefing of one of the Spaniards revealed the existence of an "insurgent mountain retreat" near Calang about four miles west of Palusapis. Apparently it was well-suited for a base camp. McRae said Calang was a basin "surrounded on all sides by high hills and entered by a narrow defile with perpendicular walls, which defile was well intrenched, both across the defile and on the side hills."

The Spaniard served as a guide to the camp. On their approach McRae's advance was fired on by insurgents and in the brief skirmish, 10 prisoners were taken. The town was deserted by the time McRae's detachment arrived "but showed evidence of recent occupation". Among the war materiel burned were four storehouses containing about three tons of rice, a large amount of medical supplies, entrenching tools and some barracks. The detachment returned to Palusapis for the night. The next day they destroyed several barracks and took a prisoner at Tibu.

The Battle of Mount Lumandan

On January 17, McRae left three squads and the mounted detachment at Palusapis but took the rest of the command back to Calang for a more thorough scout of the area. After securing the area, he left a portion of the command in Calang and took 60 men of Companies F and G, 12 Macabebe Scouts and Lieutenants Barker and Humphrey on a scout "on a dim trail leading in a southwestern direction into the mountains."

McRae reported:

> "After proceeding about 3 miles an insurgent was captured having on his person a pass given by the insurgent General Hizon,[96] dated that day. From this prisoner it was learned that General Hizon, with 50 men, was then at a mountain stronghold, called Dumandan, about 4 miles farther on. Hastening, the prisoner as guide, we followed the trail into the bed of a mountain stream, up which we followed, crossing and recrossing the stream, all traces of the trail being lost among the bowlders (sic) After continuing up the stream about a mile, the advance guard was fired upon by the enemy's outpost, concealed behind a parapet of stones in a clump of trees. The fire was promptly returned and the outpost fled, 1 rifle being captured..."[97]

The thickness of the woods allowed the outpost to retreat and McRae had trouble finding a trail that would allow an advance up the mountain. Eventually finding the main trail he took a part of his force forward to scout the advance. After going about 300

---

[96] **Hizon (28 May 1870 to 1 September 1901)** was a native of Mexico, Pampanga Province and was an early member of the Katipunan. A delegate to the Malolos Congress, he served as a Brigadier General. He stubbornly defended a portion of Caloocan in the battle there eventually retreating because the troops ran out of ammunition. He was captured in 1900 and sent to Guam where he died of a heart attack

[97] McRae's Report, No. 122, p370; the name Dumandan and Lumandan appear to reflect the same place. Lumandan is listed for the battle.

yards McRae reported,

> "a heavy fire was opened upon us from an intrenchment on the crest of the hill at the head of the ravine. The fire was returned with vigor, and, utilizing the rocks for cover, the advance approached within 50 yards of the enemy's position. The remainder of the force was then brought up by Lieutenant Barker, and a squad was sent to climb, if possible, the cliff to the left. They succeeded in gaining a position opposite and nearly on a level with the enemy's intrenchments, from which several well-directed volleys were poured into the enemy, under cover of which our men advanced to directly underneath the enemy's position, where we were comparatively sheltered from fire. The enemy's position was such that a flanking movement was impossible. I therefore ordered a direct assault, which was most gallantly made, the enemy scattering and fleeing back into the mountains. The position was accessible by one trail only, across which an intrenchment was placed at the crest of the hill, and which was so steep the men had to cling to vines and assist each other in climbing up. The enemy made a stubborn defense, keeping up a heavy fire all the time, some of them remaining in the trench until we were within a few yards. Fortunately most of their shots went high above our heads. Four insurgents, including 1 lieutenant, were killed in the trench, and several were wounded, the exact number being unknown, as they were borne away. Our casualty was one man wounded. One insurgent Captain and 1 private were taken prisoner. One hundred and thirty-seven rifles and several thousand rounds of ammunition were captured. A factory for reloading ammunition, in which was stored a large quantity of rice and some other provisions was burned. Two United States Government mules were recaptured..."[98]

---

[98] **McRae's Report, No. 122, p369-372**

McRae followed up with aggressive patrolling in the area over the next several days taking small arms fire, capturing prisoners and weapons. An action on January 19 near Banola resulted in the capture of important military papers belonging to a General Mascardo. McRae led the mounted detachment on a scout to Banaba on 24 January resulting in the capture of about 5,000 pounds of powder, ordnance material and a powder factory. The factory was destroyed. On the 28th, Lt. Barker with Company F was fired on about 30 bandits, mainly Negritos. He returned fire, wounding several but a ravine prevented pursuit. Aggressive area patrols were continued through 6 February resulting in the confiscation of arms and prisoners.

McRae reported 181 rifles captured; 95 rifles voluntarily surrendered; one brass cannon, about 6 tons of rice, 7,000 rounds of cartridges, 5,000 pounds of powder and artillery ammunition, two U.S. mules, one carriage belonging to General [Tomas] Mascardo, one quiles and one carromato captured. One powder factory and about 20 insurgent barracks and storehouses were captured and burned. Also captured were 51 insurgent prisoners. General Grant reported a saddle recovered "belonging to General [James Franklin] Bell...unintentionally loaned to Mascardo some time since. It has one bullet hole in it, but is otherwise in good condition and will be returned shortly to General Bell."[99]

While not mentioned in his report, AGO records indicate McRae's force also captured Mascardo's wife in addition to three Spanish soldiers who had been held as POWs by the Filipinos.[100]

McRae's expeditions were an unqualified success resulting in the capture of over 6,200 rounds of small arms ammunition, over 200 rounds of artillery ammunition, over 273 rifles, more than 1.5 tons of gunpowder, countless pieces of equipment, rice and other supplies and gunpowder making equipment. At least five insurgents were killed and over 50 taken prisoner to include several officers. McRae's January expeditions very nearly cleared

---

[99] Ibid; AR 1900, Part 6, p491-492, General Grant to General MacArthur, 20 January 1900
[100] *Correspondence*, (Jan. 19, 1900), 1135; Third Infantry Returns

the Third Infantry's operations area of organized guerrilla activity. For several months, the Third was involved in small unit actions.

On 7 February 1900, Captain Arthur Williams, at Malabon turned into the government treasury $322 of money taken from two insurgents near Malolos. There's no further explanation as to how it came to be seized but this and other documentation suggests there was an effort by U.S. authorities to account for seized property.[101]

In an unrelated action two men of the regiment suffered a stroke of luck when an expedition near Vigan (northwest Luzon) succeeded in recapturing 24 American soldiers from the Filipino insurgents. Among the men freed were Private Archie H. Gordon of Company K and Private George T. Sackett of Co. H.[102]

Army Reorganizes

The Army reorganized again on January 31. Though it remained in MacArthur's Division, the Third Infantry was placed in the Second Brigade, commanded by Brigadier General Frederick D. Grant. On March 29 MacArthur was given command of the Department of North Luzon.[103]

The only significant Third Infantry action during this time was on March 22 when Capt. McRae led Company E on a raid. The company left Meycauayan at 3:30 a.m. and marched to the Novaliches barrio of Ugong about 12 miles away. No resistance was encountered however 19 POWs were taken along with 64 rifles and 2000 rounds of small arms ammunition.[104]

---

[101] Elihu Root Papers, AR, Vo. 14, p273,
[102] *Correspondence,* 1128; Ibid, 1129;see also *San Francisco Chronicle,* 8 Jan 1900, p2, 'Gillmore And Men Safe in Manila'.
[103] *Correspondence,* 1154; Ibid, Table of Organizations, Appendix.
[104] Third Infantry Returns, March 1900.

U.S. WAR DEPARTMENT MAP - Dated 31 March 1900, it provides a snapshot of the locations of U.S. Army detachments during this phase of operations. Headquarters for D Company is just north of Manila along the railroad. A Detachment of Company K holds the northern end at S. Tomas.

MacArthur replaced Otis as supreme commander on May 5, 1900 and was named military governor of the Philippine Archipelago. MacArthur changed from the strict military tactics used by Otis and attempted to win the" hearts and minds" of the Philippine people by establishing an amnesty program and implementing political reforms including the guarantee of all personal liberties held by the people of the U.S. He lifted the curfew and refused to curtail freedom of speech except that which advocated the violent overthrow of the U.S. He allowed Filipino groups to meet and encouraged their political leaders to speak publicly while encouraging his officers to establish personal relationships with local Filipino leaders.[105]

The Army increased open markets, rebuilt villages, roads and schools and attempted to prepare the Filipino people for its own

---

[105] **Beede, 279.**

self-government in a program President William McKinley called "Benevolent pacification." The Filipino people took advantage of these opportunities and conditions but many continued to provide support to insurgent forces.[106]

By November 1900 the civic actions were accompanied by an aggressive counterinsurgency campaign which involved early type of "clear and hold" missions targeting guerilla strongholds and the punishment of insurgent supporters with the added element of relocating villages to U.S. zones of control.[107] The relocations were designed to isolate the people from the guerillas thereby denying the guerillas support in the form of food, shelter and money but often made daily life worse. Overpopulation created unsanitary conditions which caused disease.[108]

The summer and fall saw increases in clashes throughout the Philippines. In June, Company G was attached to the 35th Infantry. On June 4 at the barrio of Louca they encountered and routed a force of Filipino guerilas. Company H joined the unit and proceeded against a reported insurgent stronghold at Balibag on June 7 where no resistance was encountered. July saw one battle and two smaller actions involving the Third Infantry.[109]

Emilio Aguinaldo

Tempo Increases
The tempo of insurgent actions increased nationwide during the latter half of the year culminating in September and October when 241

---

[106] Ibid, 426.
[107] **General Bell concentrated villages in Batangas Province.**
[108] Ibid.
[109] **Beede, 270; Third Infantry Returns, June 1900. On June 30, 1900 the Third U.S. Infantry equated to 44 officers, 1,436 men. Table A, *AGO Report*, War Department, 1907, Vol I, Pt. III.**

total combats were counted. Aguinaldo directed the increased operations in a last major effort to influence the November U.S. Presidential election where it was hoped William Jennings Bryan, who favored Philippine independence, would defeat incumbent William McKinley.

In General Order No. 202, Aguinaldo said that during the summer the insurgents must "give such hard knocks to the Americans that they will...set in motion the fall of the Imperialist party which is trying to enslave us." On July 2 a group of about 50 ladrones (bandits) hid themselves in the steamer *Filipino* which departed Manila for a destination northward along the coast of Manila Bay. When the ship was passing the vicinity of Gotung, the ladrones revealed themselves, seized the ship and robbed all on board.[110]

Several American detachments were sent out to try to locate the bandits and included one led by District Commander General Grant. On July 2, a Third Infantry detachment of 20 men under the command of Sergeant Alfred H. Merriam, Co. H, departed the outpost at Hagonoy "to scout the surrounding country in search of the robbers of the Steamboat *Filipino*."[111]

According to reports the Americans stayed overnight at Tibaguin in native boats leaving that place at about 6 a.m. on July 3 "intending to return to Hagonoy. When about one and one-half miles north of Tibaguin on the Tibaguin River the detachment was attacked by 80 to 110 insurgents armed with Remington and Mauser rifles concealed in the nipa on both sides of the river."[112]

The report said, "Privates [Charles] Gaddy and [Herman] Burdt were wounded by the first volley. The detachment immediately landed and charged the enemy but a converging fire from three directions soon forced it to take the defensive." Sergeant Merriam was shot in the neck and killed instantaneously.[113]

---

[110] Wolf, 322; Congressional Record, *Narrative History*, 118.
[111] Congressional History, *Narrative History*, 118; Third Infantry Returns, July 1900.
[112] Third Infantry Returns, July 1900; Ibid, Report of Engagement, 1900.
[113] Ibid, Returns; Ibid, Report of Engagement, 1900.

Corporal Frank Wallace took command "as soon as Sergeant Merriam was killed, and with his detachment gallantly charging and driving back a force of the armed natives, four or five times greater in number than his own." The action lasted till 10:30 a.m. when the approach of a detachment of Company I, Third Infantry under Lt. [John H.] Page [Jr.] forced the enemy to withdraw."[114]

Six rifles were captured and six more were destroyed and thrown into the river. Gaddy later died of his wounds. A third man was also killed with two others wounded. At least 12 enemy were killed and the remainder dispersed. For his actions that day, Corporal Wallace was recommended for the Congressional Medal of Honor. This was downgraded to the Certificate of Merit.[115]

Also on July 3, a detachment from Company G was fired on while on patrol in the river. One American was killed and two wounded. One Mauser rifle and 200 rounds of ammunition were captured. The night of July 27 at Polo, an outpost of Company E was fired on without casualties.[116]

The month of August remained quiet but the latter half of September saw four actions. Polo was the focus of a concentrated insurgent attack on Sept. 16. In that action an estimated 125 insurgents attacked Company E's 20 man outpost. No casualties were reported. The same day at Company G's outpost at Guiguinto, a 20-man platoon under the command of 1Lt H.A. Smith was attacked by between 75 and 300 insurgents at 12:15 a.m. According to reports, "the firing, which was heavy, lasted until about 1 a.m." Locals told the Americans that insurgent losses included three killed and a number of wounded. Two Americans were wounded but not seriously.[117]

---

[114] Ibid, Returns; Ibid, Report of Engagement, 1900.
[115] Third Infantry Returns, July 1900; Congressional Record, Narrative History, 118; AGO OR, F&S, Index; AGO General Orders, GO86, July 24, 1902; see also *New York Daily Tribune*, Sunday, February 16, 1902, page 12. 'The Army's Roll of Honor – List of Awards for Gallantry in Cuba, the Philippines and China'.
[116] Third Infantry Returns, 1900
[117] Third Infantry Returns, Sept. 1900; Ibid, Report of Engagement.

On Sept. 20 a detachment of 37 men from Companies F and L and under 2nd Lt. George Lewis surprised and captured a key insurgent arsenal and munitions shop hidden in a swamp. Lewis's group engaged the insurgents in a swamp just south of Atlog killing three insurgents and taking nine prisoners. They also took nine Filipino boats, seven rifles, 3,000 rounds of ammunition, thousands of shells, 100 pounds of sheet brass, 1,000 pounds of rice, powder, official insurgent papers and a sum of money including gold specie. The Americans destroyed "the arsenal" and equipment which was used for repairing weapons. They also destroyed eleven buildings including the headquarters and personal effects of one guerilla leader identified as Torres. One American was wounded in the operation. Three days later Capt. McRae with a 25-man element of Company E surprised and captured 26 guerillas in a barracks at Bahay Pari. The Americans recovered 22 Remington rifles and 300 rounds of small arms ammunition. Two insurgents were wounded when they tried to escape.[118]

Small unit actions continued through October. On October 4, Lt. Sharp, commanding a detachment of Company A was on a scout near La Lombay when they engaged and captured three 'ladrones' and two rifles. They destroyed an insurgent barracks and 800 pounds of rice. On October 10, Lt. Moore with a detachment of 50 men proceeded down the Clanta River to attack an insurgent tax collection station one mile below Atlong. Two insurgents were wounded and one was captured along with a revolver and insurgent papers. Two weeks later on October 24 General Grant and a party of officers narrowly avoided an insurgent ambush while visiting the Third Infantry in Dinalupijan. Grant was informed the insurgents were "lying in wait for them at the barrio Avon." Lt. Humphrey and twelve men from the Third took off on horseback serving as Grant's advance. They engaged 18 insurgents near the barrio killing nine without taking a single casualty.[119]

---

[118] Third Infantry Returns, September 1900; Ibid, Report of Engagement.; *Annual Report of the War Department, 1901*, Part 5, Appendix M, *'Report of Major General Lloyd Wheaton, U.S.A., Command Department of North Luzon, [01 August 1900] to June 30, 1901'*, 279., hereafter, **Appendix M.**
[119] **(Appendix M, 280-282)**

The Third took casualties in November. On the 11th, Lt. George Lewis led his men on a recon in the swamps near Santa Cruz where they discovered three insurgent barracks. They attacked killing three guerillas and wounding one. They burned the barracks and eight boats. On November 21, a detachment of Company M, while on a routine scout, struck a party of guerillas near Taliptip near Bulacan. They captured two and wounded two. On November 22, a 39-man detachment commanded by Lt. Lewis, consisting of men from Companies F & I, were on patrol in boats in the Calante [Punaran]River near Malolos when they were ambushed by ladrones near the barrio of Masili. The Americans were fired on at close range with a single volley and then the bandits fled. One American was killed and two were wounded.[120]

Nothing again happened until December 2 when General Grant, commanding a detachment of the Third, "cleaned out Candaba Swamp west of Malolos, having a couple of skirmishes." They captured six rifles and 2,000 rounds of ammunition. On 9 December, 1st Lt. Ralph Hagsdall commanded 45 to 50 men from Companies H and E. They depart La Lombay about 2 p.m. and struck an insurgent outpost near the village of Loma de Gato. The Americans engaged about 200 insurgents in a one hour battle "driving him across the country for about one hour when the enemy scattered." The Americans pursued for about two hours before calling off the attack. Nine insurgents were killed and six were wounded. Among the dead was the insurgent commander, Captain Morales, brother of an insurgent Colonel. There were no U.S. casualties. The patrol returned to camp about 8 p.m.[121]

The year was hard for Filipinos working with the Third Infantry. One report states "two natives who acted as guides for American troops of [Maycauayan] disappeared afterwards, one in April and the other September 25…rumors indicate they were killed."

Government sources show three incidents occurring over the

---

[120] Third Infantry Returns, October 1900; Ibid, November 1900; Ibid, Report of Engagement; Appendix M, 284-85.
[121] Third Infantry Returns, December 1900. Appendix M, 285-286.

course of three days in December. On 10 December, at Lolomboy, the presidente of Bocaze was assassinated "on account of his sympathy with the Americans". The next day at Apalit, two natives "Francisco Salaveria and Telesforo Ponce were assassinated for suspected sympathy and assistance to the American cause. These men…had given information against the insurgents and thieves" to the American authorities. On 12 December, at San Fernando, "the alcalde of Angeles, Florentina Paminapuan, a rich man, had been formerly carried away and required to pay a ransom of 9,000 pesos."[122]

Unidentified Army Patrol in 1900

---

[122] *Charges of Cruelty, etc., to the Natives of the Philippines: Letter from the Secretary of War Relative to the Reports and Charges in the Public Press of Cruelty and Oppression Exercised by Our Soldiers Toward Natives of the Philippines'*, 57th Congress, U.S. Senate, 1st Session, Doc. No. 205, Part 1 **(Washington: GPO) 1902.**

General Arthur MacArthur

CHAPTER 6
LUZON OPERATIONS OF 1901

The combination of civic action programs and aggressive Army counterinsurgency operations split the Philippine people who saw the American occupiers in a different light than their former Spanish landlords. The middle and upper classes were tired of the war and saw social and economic progress and the promise of eventual independence under the American flag. They wanted peace.

The American was taking root. Filipino forces, such as the Philippine Constabulary and Macabebe Scouts, organized under U.S. commanders, served side-by-side with U.S. regulars and were soon conducting counterinsurgency operations on their own. The constant military pressure, coupled with the civic action programs (sometimes characterized as a 'carrot and stick' approach) had the desired effect. In the Third Infantry area of operations, some guerillas voluntarily surrendered 112 rifles and 1500 rounds of ammo on February 13, 1901. MacArthur reported most of the material had been hidden in nearby swamps. He said the incident was important in that it showed the locals were favorable to the Americans in Bulacan Province which was previously "one of the worst in Luzon. [The] Result accomplished exclusively by long-continued, intelligent, persistent efforts [by the] officers of the Third U.S. Infantry."

Aggressive American patrols continued to take a toll on the guerilas. On February 23, Lt. Lewis was scouting the nipa swamps between Santa Cruz and the Calante River when he came in contact with ladrones. They engaged three times that day and twice more the next. Lewis was successful in killing guerilla Captain Amolate Alonzo, capturing two rifles and 275 rounds of ammunition without any American casualties.[123]

The Third Infantry's Bulacan was where a "dramatic episode" was witnessed by a *New York Times* reporter covering on the March organization of Filipino Provincial Governments. He wrote;

> *"Bulacan was considered the centre of the insurrection. Its inhabitants are pure Tagalogs, active fighters in war, and apparently so from the start in politics. Malolos, it's most populous and centrally situated town, according to common repute, still gloried in having been the seat of Aguinaldo's capital and its people still surreptitiously opposed surrender to American authority.*
>
> *"To the people of Bulacan and especially to the delegates from the Malolos district, the sessions of the (U.S. Philippine Commission) were a revelation. They came cowed and curious, and departed many of them with tears in their eyes, full of confident hopes for the*

---

[123] *Correspondence,* (Feb. 15, 1901), 1254; Appendix M, 293.

> *future of their country. To them such hopes were indeed a new sensation after the years of harassing, dogged, practically hopeless warfare. The frank, fair statements of the representatives of the President of the United States impressed them mightily. They came in factions, chiefly imbued with the idea of landing their respective candidates in the provincial offices; they left satisfied with the results and with American principles."*[124]

On this occasion insurgent General Flores said,

> *"It is true that I was not long since in the field against America. But I became convinced that that was not the way to obtain our liberties. In so saying I do not feel that I am in the least degree deserting my oath taken to the Government of Malolos. I regard my oath to the Government of the United States now as but a repetition of my oath at Malolos, for the ideals in my mind were and are identical. I do not expect from this people the submission of slaves, but the common sense which is necessary to the success of popular government."*[125]

The Filipino delegates debated, discussed and voted on Malolos as the provincial capital. The first Filipino governor chosen was former insurgent leader Jose Serapio, uncle of Aguinaldo. Several other former insurgent leaders were also appointed to positions of responsibility illustrating the American government did not intend to treat them as the Spanish had.

One former guerilla said, "The starry flag which waves above us cannot be the emblem of oppression. The American Government has shown by the establishment of free schools that it never intended enslaving us." He called for the immediate implementation of a land tax so the Filipino people could help pay

---

[124] **NYT, May 31, 1901.**
[125] **Ibid.**

for their own efforts at self-government.[126]

District Commander General F.D. Grant was asked to pronounce the benediction at the service and, in a dramatic moment, took the American flag and draped it over the shoulders of Governor-elect Serapio, "charging the new Governor, his people, and their children to respect, fight for and defend that flag, which was to float over the home of the Governor of Bulacan and, figuratively, over all loyal citizens of the province. All present were deeply affected by this impromptu climax, and many native wept unrestrainedly. The impressive scene ended with a charge by [Philippine Commission President William Howard] Taft that the new officers exercise their authority with malice toward none, with charity for all."[127]

The report continued, "It is regarded as a singular fact that of the five provinces first organized, the one whose patriotism to America was most in doubt should be the scene of such sincere enthusiams for American sovereignty...the sincerity and enthusiasm of the Bulacan Tagologs, when once they had grasped the true purport of American institutions and intentions, were far from being equaled."

The fighting was not over however. The Third Infantry was engaged in five actions in March. On March 3, Sgt. Eliot D. Reynolds, Co. A, engaged insurgent forces north of Bigaa. His patrol captured four men belonging to "Biloz's band" as well as one rifle. On the same day, Captain Kilbourne "with a detachment of native scouts from Malolos struck [a] band of six insurgents while searching for rifles in barrio Looc." They killed three insurgents including the commander, Captain Jacob Santos. On March 16, Lt. William R. Gibson, Co. M was on a scout with four men and encountered ten insurgents under Biloz. The Americans initiated an attack and chased the guerillas capturing four along with three rifles and a revolver. On March 19, Capt. James J. McRae led 35 men of Company E on a scout when they "discovered 25 armed insurgents on the south bank of the Marilao

---

[126] **Ibid.**
[127] **Ibid.**

River one mile west of Presna." The Americans attacked killing two insurgents, wounding one and capturing one. They also took two rifles and 50 rounds of ammunition. Two more insurgents were killed on March 25 when Lt. Lewis, commanding a detachment of Company I on patrol, engaged guerillas southwest of Atlog.[128]

Aguinaldo was captured in late March of 1901. The combination of American pacification programs, Aguinaldo's capture and his eventual calls for peace and the end of resistance pretty much ended the organized rebellion though pockets of resistance continued to exist.

There were still some minor combats and the last on record for the Third Infantry in Luzon occurred about one month after the organization of the Provincial government. On April 18, 1901, Captain James H. McRae led a 39 man detachment of Companies F and G into the jungles of Luzon east of Norzagary "for [the] purpose of punishing insurgents under Torres." They engaged the enemy on April 19 killing one and capturing several others along with several rifles. In a second action on April 21, more rifles were captured. The detachment returned to base on April 22 for a net haul of six rifles, one revolver, 50 rounds of ammunition and guerila papers. Two insurgents were killed, two wounded and four captured during the operation.[129]

On April 25, elements of Company G on patrol near Norzagary engaged Filipino guerilas. The Americans pressed the insurgents killing five. They captured 25 rifles, a Filipino officer and 13 men. Soon after this, Filipino General Morres and six of his remaining men appeared in Norzagary to surrender to the detachment. Later, General Moreales surrendered. These were the last combat actions of 'the Old Guard' in the Philippine Insurrection.[130]

---

[128] Appendix M, 293-295.
[129] Third Infantry Returns, April 1901; Appendix M, 296; see also *Annual Report, FY Ended June 30, 1901*, Part 2.
[130] NYT, May 31, 1901, p5; Third Infantry Returns, April 1901; The Third Infantry's Lt. A.U. Faulkner of Company C would lead two Macabebe Scout operations in December but no U.S. troops appear to have supported.

A general amnesty was offered through May 1901. This deadline was later extended. That same month, outgoing Bulacan Province Commander Grant told the *New York Times*:

> "I can tell you that peace and quietness prevail throughout the archipelago except in two or three districts. The center of the disturbance is in the southern part of Luzon, the Batanzas, and adjacent territory. The latter may best be referred to as shoe-string districts of mountainous territory. [Filipino] Generals Cailles and Malvar are making most of the trouble. They control the robber bands operating there. Malvar has proclaimed himself dictator. But he is not doing so much dictating as running away from American troops...There has been nothing worthy of the name of warfare since the end of 1899. We have, since that time, had nothing but roving bands to deal with. In the territory where I was in command the rebellion is entirely wiped out." [131]

The Military Government transferred total administration of the islands to the civilian Philippine Commission on July 4, 1901. The Third Infantry spent the rest of the year in routine camp duties, uneventful patrols and serving as train guards. The latter half of the 1901 saw detachments abandoning minor outposts and turning over major positions to local Philippine Scouts.

There was at least one altercation with local civil government in the Third Infantry area or responsibility in the fall of 1901 that required intervention.[132] On October 31, a U.S. informant and employee named Fausto Bihasa was ordered arrested by the Provincial Governor Serapio of Bulacan. The Maximo de Jesus, justice of the peace of the pueblo of Santa Maria, had a warrant in which Bihasa was accused of "offenses against the authorities of others". Once arrested, his transfer to a civil jail was stopped by the local U.S. commander Lt. Philip E. M. Walker who directed the prisoner retained in Santa Maria... The Filipino authorities

---

[131] **NYT, May 31, 1901.**
[132] **This event is detailed in the April 1902 hearings of the U.S. Senate Philippine Commission, Vol. 3, pages 2180 to 2190.**

protested the matter with Luke E. Wright, Acting Civil Governor of the Philippine Islands who referred the matter, on 19 November, to the U.S. Commander and Military Governor. The issue was sent back down the military chain of command to Walker, commanding officer at Santa Maria and Bihasa's rescuer. Walker responded on 2 December with a full report.

His report revealed Bihasa had been Chief of Police under the military authorities and had been appointed to the position at the recommendation of Captain McRae and an officer of the 35th USV Infantry, formerly commanding the station because Bihasa "belonged to none of the various parties of this neighborhood, and therefore could be relied upon to do his duty against whomsoever, which he did faithfully and well and often at his own peril. During his entire term he rendered most excellent service in capturing arms and ladrones."

Walker noted that just prior to the shift from military to civil control, an incident occurred "which added greatly to the enmity of the governor toward Chief Bihasa…on the previous night a number of carabaos had been stolen from the people of [Norzagary] by ladrones from [Santa Maria] who were supposed to be under the protection of the civil governor." One of the animals was in the possession of the governor's family. Walker sent Bihasa to investigate discovered the governor's sister had it. Walker reported the "owner has positively identified it as his property. As the people in whose possession it was could not account to my satisfaction, I ordered [Bihasa] to return it to its owner." Bihasa feared retribution by the Governor and Walker offered protection as Bihasa was doing his lawful duty. Walker said, "From this time on he has been persecuted by the governor."

U.S military authorities also directed Bihasa and a squad of police to seize weapons from the Governor and his friends. The Governor charged Bihasa after this event and ordered his arrest and movement to Malolos. Walker refused to release Bihasa for his safety reporting Bihasa "expressed great fear and begged me not to allow him to be marched to Malolos, as he feared they intended to get him off in the fields and then kill him. As I also entertained grave doubts as to the sincerity of this expedition, I ordered the presidente [of Santa Maria] to keep him in confinement here for the time being."

Lt. Walker reported Bihasa "was actively but secretly opposed by the provincial governor, who caused me much annoyance by giving order secretly to the police contrary to my wishes and the orders of the Chief Bihasa, and therefore often defeating my plans." The Chief U.S. Constable in Manila, for whom Bihasa worked, was made aware of the situation. The Chief Constable asked Bihasa be sent to Manila immediately. Walker got Bihasa out of jail, loaned him a revolver and directed to him to report to Manila.

Walker reported the Bihasa issue:

> *"was a pure case of persecution amounting in its nature to blackmail. This fact is well known to all the officers and men that were cognizant of the local conditions...I considered it my first and all-important duty to protect the only entirely loyal and disinterested native of my acquaintance, and the man that carried out my orders without regard to his personal safety or hope of pecuniary advantage. Fausto Bihasa is the victim of malicious persecution, and his only crime is that he does not belong to the provincial governor's party, and could not be intimidated or coerced by [the Governor] into a life of double dealing...The people of this town are now watching with a great deal of interest to see whether the Americans are going to support and protect the man who has "stuck" to them through thick and thin, or whether they are going to allow him to be persecuted by a man [the Governor] whose duplicity and abuse of power is the common talk of this section of the province."*

Colonel Page concurred in his endorsement noting, "Suspicion of duplicity has for a long time attached to the governor of Bulacan Province. I therefore sustain and commend the action of Lieutenant Walker, and recommend that in justice to the military the conduct of this governor be thoroughly investigated. It would seem to be a very inopportune time for the civil government to hold the upper hand over the military, especially when the former is administered by such a man as the governor of Bulacan is generally believed to be, as unscrupulous civil officials would have it in their power to persecute at will, as in this case, natives friendly to the Americans and loyal to the American Government."

On 12 December, U.S. Military Commander Major General Adna R. Chaffee, in concurring, told U.S. Civil Governor Wright that "I must insist upon adequate protection being afforded Fausto Bihasa before releasing him from the protection of military authorities."

On 20 December, a lengthy response was sent to Chaffee from Wright, the Vice-Civil Governor and, at the time, the Acting Civil Governor, protesting military interference with a civil affair. The note reflects tensions between the U.S. civilian government and the U.S. military authorities policing the region. Wright argued that no one had previously claimed Governor Serapio was corrupt and the military officers had exceeded their authority. He argued that U.S. civil authorities were in control of the Philippines now and the military should not interfere in the adjudication of civil law. He argued that Bihasa should be remanded to civil custody.

Chaffee responded two days later, advising him that Bihasa had already been released.

The safety provided by the small detachments of the Third Infantry in village outposts appears to have endeared them to some local citizens according to documents showing Filipinos requesting the retention of U.S. troops in their villages. As the Third Infantry was abandoning outposts, the natives of Obando and Bulacan formally petitioned for the retention of troops. The natives of Santa Maria, San Miguel and Polo verbally expressed a "hope that American troops would not be withdrawn".[133] In reporting these developments to his superiors, Colonel Page said, "The same

---

[133] Colonel Page, Third Infantry, Malabon, Rizal to Adjutant General, Second Brigade, San Fernando, 12 February 1902. Contained in *Hearings*, p.1823.

sentiments have been expressed to me by prominent natives of Malabon, and I believe that sentiment generally on part of all native lovers of peace and good order." Page noted the citizens likely did not have the initiative or courage to make a formal petition, in part, due to fear of former insurrectionists placed into civil office by the Federal Party.

The regiment was ordered to concentrate at Camp Wallace, Manila on March 12, 1902 in preparation for going home. They embarked on the U.S. transport *Thomas* on March 17, set sail at 1 p.m. on March 18 and arrived in San Francisco at 11 a.m. on April 15 or three years, two and one-half months after leaving New York. [134]

For all intents and purposes, the insurrection was over. President Teddy Roosevelt declared it so as of July 4, 1902.

Conspicuous Service
It should be noted that prior to World War I, the U.S. Army recognized conspicuous service with letters of recognition, a Certificate of Merit and the Medal of Honor which was the only personal medal authorized at the time though campaign medals and marksmanship awards were in existence.[135] The Third Infantry Regiment was not without its heroes in the Philippines.

Records indicate a number of men were recognized with letters or certificates of merit and at least one man was nominated for the Congressional Medal of Honor. Among those recognized with a Certificate of Merit were:

- Frank Wallace   Corporal Co. H
  May 13, 1899

- William H. Deavey   Sergeant Co. H
  Dec. 3, 1899

---

[134] Third Infantry Returns, March 902; Ibid, April 1902.
[135] John J. Pershing, My Experiences In the First World War, (New York: Da Capo Press, 1995), 341-342. In World War I, Congress created the Distinguished Service Cross, the Distinguished Service Medal and the Silver Star. The award of the Certificate of Merit was discontinued sometime after this time.

- Martin J. Murphy   Artificer Co. B
  Jan. 23, 1900

- Otto Scheu   Corporal Co. B
  April 15, 1900

- Patrick Kaine   Private Co. D
  Oct. 11, 1900

Among these heroes are many others that did not return.[136]

The 'Old Guard' was involved in over 100 combat actions ranging from battles to more minor scrapes. There were over 20 combat related deaths, over 60 wounded, several became prisoners of war and many others died of disease aggravated by hard campaigning in an unfriendly tropical environment.

Historian Michael Clodfelter said, "The Filipino Insurrection has been treated by American history books as but a minor military irritant. It was not considered so at the time, however. For it required a major deployment of American resources and men and it caused deep divisions between those Americans who supported the war and those who opposed it, much like the internal dissension brought about later by a Southeast Asian war in which the United States found itself embroiled."[137]

---

[136] **AGO OR, F&S, Index. for Murphy, Sheu and Kaine; A log entry from August 18, 1900 calls for** *"additional remarks to be appended to the 'Record of Events' for July 1900 in the case of Corporal Frank Wallace, Company H, recommended for Medal of Honor."*; **AGO General Orders, GO #86, July 24, 1902 for Wallace for** *"most distinguished gallantry in action at San Miquel de Mayumo, Luzon, Philippine Islands, May 13, 1899."* **Awarded March 16, 1902. Wallace was discharged March 25, 1900.; AGO General Orders, GO#107, July 1, 1905, for Deavey for "gallant conduct, while a Sergeant, Co. H Third U.S. Infantry, during the operations of General Grant in the Philippine Islands in December 1899, particularly the night of December 3, 1899, when he, without a moment's hesitation, plunged into the Almacenes River, near Hermosa, P.I., the night being dark and the water deep, and with the assistance of others managed, after much hard work, to get a large raft into a position which enabled the rest of the command to cross." [316586AGO].**

[137] **Clodfelter, 418-419.**

Home Again

Private John Hix was discharged from the Army on December 29, 1901 with his three years of service characterized as being "honest and faithful." He was one of 126,458 American soldiers who served during the insurrection. Of that number 4,243 died; 1,073 killed in battle and the remainder dead of disease or other causes. Another 2,218 were wounded in battle.

Hix married Lura Emma Soper on December 19, 1904 and had nine children, 14 grandchildren and 15 great-grandchildren. Daughter Mildred Echols related that her father was paid a pension for many years because of his Philippine service, perhaps as the result of a sickness that hospitalized him while here.

In August 1976, at the age of 102, Hix was blind but his mental capacity and sense of humor were characterized as quite good. According to one of his nurses at that time, "Mr. Hix is one of the most popular residents and is the oldest resident in the home." He died about six months later. He was perhaps the last Philippine-American war veteran of "the Old Guard."[138]

---

[138] **The Crewe-Burkeville Journal.**

Wartime Drawing by Russian artist Vasili Verestchagin

Crime and Punishment

The service of ordinary American soldiers in the Philippine War has been negatively portrayed over the years by the politicalization of U.S. involvement there. These impressions were fostered at the time by "anti-imperialists" who felt the U.S. should not be a global power with territories. Criticisms were further fueled by the brutal actions of a few field commanders whose excessive wartime policies led to needless civilian deaths.[139] It was further distorted during the Vietnam War by activists attempting to draw comparisons between the conflicts to further their political objectives. In both instances the U.S. soldier was subjected to some level of vilification. An honest examination suggests the service of the ordinary U.S. soldier, with notable exceptions, was honorable.[140]

The U.S. military was and is a cross-section of American society. As a result, unsavory characters will occasionally pass through its

---

[139] Specifically Brigadier General Jacob H. Smith whose brutal Samar campaign led to his court martial and Brigadier General James Franklin Bell whose retaliations resulted in the deaths of thousands of Filipinos.
[140] No attempt is made here to address or debate U.S. policy of that era.

ranks where they will continue to engage in morally offensive practices, sometimes criminal in nature, to the detriment of the reputation of honest soldiers and the uniform they wear. The purpose of this essay is not to explore war crimes or atrocities but only to document war crimes and crime as it involved the Third U.S. Infantry in the Philippines.

The Third Infantry was not without its disciplinary problems, generally desertions. Most of these occurred as the unit was about to deploy to the Philippines and there was a spike just as the unit was preparing to return to the United States suggesting many of those stationed in the Philippines did not want to leave. Most of the desertions appear to have been remedied through unit level discipline though several men faced General Court Martial (GCM) and were dishonorably discharged from service.

There is documentation of two serious crimes committed by members of the regiment. The first of these occurred during the Malolos Campaign. Private William E. Scarborough, Company B, Third Infantry was charged with a violation of the laws of war occurring on 21 April 1899. He was charged with rape and "disorderly conduct to the prejudice of good order and military discipline". The charges specified Scarborough "did, without permission or authority, enter the house of peaceable Filipino residents of the island of Novotas, near Manila, P.I. and terrify men, women and children by discharging his rifle into and around their houses." As specified, Scarborough also "did criminally assault and commit rape upon the person of Aldiana Dionisia, a middle-aged Filipino woman, in a house on the island of Novotas, near Manila, P.I."

Scarborough pled not guilty to both charges but a military court determined otherwise and he was sentenced to death. Because it was capital punishment, the President had final review. The case was sent forward and on 16 December, President McKinley commuted the death sentence to a dishonorable discharge, forfeiture of all pay and allowances and confinement at hard labor in a Federal penitentiary for the period of twenty years.[141]

In the second incident, Private John S. Anderson, Company A, Third Infantry, sometime in July 1900, did loot local civilians. Following General Court Martial he was given a dishonorable discharge, forfeiture of pay and one year confinement.[142]

Third Infantry Officers served on military courts conducting trials of bandits, also known as ladrones, who worked their area of operations. The ladrones normally targeted civilians. The documentation illustrates the efforts military authorities took to ensure the safety and security of the population through punishment of criminal offenders. There were also trials for insurgent personnel who conducted operations against U.S. forces in a manner contrary to what were then the accepted laws of war.

Incidents involving bandit crimes against the civilian population include the following:

1 January to June 1900 – Isabello del Rosario, one of "1st Lieutenant" Alejandrino's[143] men, engaged in murder and rape. Rosario admitted to killing Leonacio Torres of Porac by burying him alive. Rosario claimed Torres was "an American secret service man" trying to collect intelligence on the insurgents. Rosario also admitted to participating in the three-man gang rape of a young girl, kidnapping, terrorizing, molesting and extorting money from civilians. He was hanged by the neck until dead on 5

---

[141] Details in *Affairs in the Philippine Island: Hearings before the Committee U.S. Congress.* **Senate. Committee on the Philippines Vol 3, p2099-2100; General No 208, General Court Martial convening at Balinag,PI pursuant to FO No. 97, HQ Second Division, 8th Army Corps, San Fernando PI, 7 June 1899, Capt William C. Buttler was president and 1st Lt James T. Moore, Judge Advocate.; see also page 991,** *Affairs in the Philippine Islands, Hearings Before the Committee on the Philippines* **57th Congress, 1st Session, Senate April 10 , 1902 (Washington: GPO) 1902, Doc. 331 Part 2**
[142] Ibid, *Affairs in the Philippine Islands*, 57th Congress, 1st Session, p992, *Memorandum Showing Trials of Officers and Enlisted Men.*
[143] There was a Philippine Insurgent General named Jose Alejandrino however it is not certain this is the same man referenced. Alejandrino authored <u>The Price of Freedom: Episodes and Anecdotes of Our Struggles for Freedom</u>. (1949). He was also a member of the Malolos Congress.

April 1901. Accomplices Jacinto Pineda and Domingo Bautista received sentences of life at hard labor.[144]

30 May 1900 – Ezekiel Ignacio and Benito Lubao, working for a bandit chief, attempted to kidnap with a revolver, Proceso Mercado of Bustos. Mercado resisted and was shot. In a November 1901 trial his killers were sentenced to death by hanging.[145]

September 1900 – Outlaws under the command of insurgent 1st Lt J. Alejandrino kidnapped and killed at least two men by burying them alive. Eusebio Rojas was specifically tried for killing Dalmatio Sicat and Benacio Pamintuan of barrio Guagua. They entered town in civilian clothes to kidnap the men and buried them in the forest. The record states witnesses related "the horrible details by which men in the full vigor of life were suffocated under the mass of earth thrown upon them." Another man was murdered when Rojas ordered his men to fire on a civilian train on 30 March 1900. In other instances he tried to extort money from civilians. Rojas claimed he was "just following orders". He was found guilty and hanged on 1 March 1901.[146]

2 October 1900 – Atanacio Gatlabayan was murdered by Maximo Maricaban and Felciano Samson. Their September 1901 military trial found the victim and one of the killers were "rivals for the favor of a woman". The victim was ambushed, boloed to death and left in the rice fields. The trial acquitted Samson but found Maricaban guilty and sentenced to death, later commuted to life at hard labor.[147]

31 October 1900 – Insurgent Sergeant Luis Bernabe and a group of outlaws murder Francisco Pascual and Cayetano Pascual "by striking them, and causing them to be struck, with bolos". The two

---

[144] Ibid, p1137; p1151; p1166; Third Infantry Lt Col Greenleaf A. Goodale was President of the court and Capt. William R. Sample was judge advocate.

[145] Ibid, p1304; Third Infantry Capt James H. McRae was President of the court and 2nd Lt Robert I. Rees was judge advocate.

[146] Ibid, p1112; Third Infantry Lt Col Greenleaf A. Goodale was President of the court and Capt. William R. Sample was judge advocate.

[147] *Affairs in the Philippine Island: Hearings before the Committee U.S. Congress.* Senate. Committee on the Philippines Vol 3, p1276.

victims were friendly to the Americans. Bernabe and his group kidnapped the two victims from their homes, took them to an insurgent camp and there "stabbed them to death". Captain James McRae was president of the military commission trying Bernabe a year later on 26 October 1901. The commission wrote:

> *"The seizure of peaceful native in their homes and murdering them merely because they are accused by some evil-minded persons of being Americanistas is not war but wanton assassination. The commanding general owes to all law-abiding men the most effective means in his power for their protection, and the warning, often given, is repeated that all who order and all who engage in the murder of men friendly to the Americans or for any other unlawful motive must expect the extreme penalty of the law. No mitigating circumstances appear of record in this case nor doubt of the criminal responsibility of this accused as a principal for the crime charged."*

Bernabe was sentenced to death and publicly hanged on 22 November 1901.[148]

3 November 1900 – Asevero Tablan, Proilan Sera Josip and Platon Sacdalan with four others kidnapped Quiterio Hernandez from his home in Paombong, carried him off in a banca boat and took him to an insurgent barracks where he was killed three days later by bolo. He was buried in a newly made grave excavated "on the spot for that purpose". Tablan was hanged, Josip got life at hard labor and Sacdalan got five years in prison.[149]

1 December 1900 – Dioncio Jumaquio and Selvino Pangan, outlaws, kidnapped and murdered on Marianno Cruz of the barrio Capitangan. They were assisted by five others. The record states Cruz "was afflicted with a swelling on the back of his neck, which

---

[148] Ibid, p1293; 2nd Lt Rees was judge advocate.
[149] Ibid, p1337; Surgeon Major William H. Cook was President of the Board and 1st Lt Paul Giddings, Third Infantry Battalion Adjutant, was judge advocate.

appears to have created the impression that he was a witch, with power, by occult methods [could] make cocoanuts and eggs grow in people's bodies." Cruz was kidnapped, bound and carried away to a nearby river where he was beaten with clubs, the butt of a rifle and stabbed with a dagger. His body was thrown in river but later recovered and identified. The two men were convicted and sentenced to death. The department commander granted clemency "in view of the gross ignorance and superstition of these accused" and the killers were imprisoned at hard labor for ten years.[150]

Among the cases where U.S personnel were victims, are the following:

1 June 1899 – Near Bocaue an unidentified American soldier was killed by Gabino de la Cruz with a bolo when the soldier "was asleep in the street and in a helpless condition from intoxication." After the murder, de la Cruz got help in cleaning the crime scene and got the body to a banca boat. He took the body "down river and toward the open sea" at night to dispose of it. His commuted sentence was 30 years hard labor.[151]

13 July 1900 – Insurgent officers, dressed as civilians, lay in ambush within American lines at barrio Talipapa. First Lieutenant Richard H. Brewer and a Private Gallagher of the 27th U.S. Volunteer Infantry were riding on the road when the insurgents opened fire. The Americans dismounted and ran for shelter. When resistance appeared no longer an option the men dropped their pistols and raised their arms "in sign of surrender". They were surrounded, taken about 50 yards away, stripped of their clothes and made to kneel. One of the prisoners was murdered by being stabbed in the back with a dagger and the other was shot with a pistol from behind. On 4 November 1901, four officers of the insurgent Army – Major Agapito Ygnacio, Manuel Lerma, Lt.

---

[150] Ibid, p1315; Surgeon Major William H. Cook was President of the Board and 1st Lt Paul Giddings, Third Infantry Battalion Adjutant, was judge advocate.
[151] Ibid, 1376; Surgeon Major William H. Cook was President of the Board and 1st Lt Paul Giddings, Third Infantry Battalion Adjutant, was judge advocate.

Pio Sadalan and Lt. Benito Clemor – were sentenced to life in prison at hard labor.[152]

3 October 1900 – Insurgent Lieutenant Emilio Maria murdered Private Charles A. Baker, Company A, 35th Infantry Regiment, then a prisoner of war in the hands of Maria. The incident occurred near barrio Ylogbacod in Bulacan. The public record states Maria and his companions, while in the ordinary dress of noncombatants "kidnapped in the streets an American soldier, and taking him to a safe distance, the accused, with a rifle, shot his prisoner and caused him to be buried. The accused, upon his trial admitted facts making him clearly a principal in this wanton murder, and the weight of the testimony of eyewitnesses leaves no reasonable doubt that he conceived, as well as executed it. He was hanged on 23 Dec 1901 at Baliuag[153]

29 September 1900 – Mariano Cruz and Marcelino Trapiel of the barrio of San Vicente, Malolos murdered Corporal Crestof A. Fiedler, Company F, Third Infantry. Fiedler was the Provost Sergeant for that barrio. It appears Corporal Fiedler was zealous in the conduct of his duties. This created some friction with the local population as well as the insurgents. The court record said it appeared Fiedler "made himself obnoxious to the insurgents operating in the vicinity of Malolos because of the manner in which he, as an acting provost-sergeant, enforced sanitary regulations, and of his watchfulness of the insurgents stealing into the barrio of San Vicente in the dress of peaceful amigos."

The local insurgent leader was General Isidoro Torres. It was in this capacity that Fiedler's zealousness was called to his "special attention" through "the complaints of the people of Malolos concerning the manner in which [Fiedler] enforced sanitary regulations" and because Fiedler was

---

[152] Ibid, 1373; Surgeon Major William H. Cook was President of the Board and 1st Lt Paul Giddings, Third Infantry Battalion Adjutant, was judge advocate.

[153] Ibid, p1374; McRae was President and 2nd Lt O.H. Dockery was judge advocate.

> "*noted for his watchfulness of strangers coming into Malolos, and in calling upon them [to] give an account of their business; whereby he caused the insurgent soldiery—who in the guise of amigos visited the pueblo—much inconvenience in their constant efforts to secretly secure supplies and to gain information regarding the movements and objects of the American troops. In a single instance, in making arrests of such disguised insurgents, the arrested man broke away from his captors, ran, and refusing to halt, was shot down by the decedent, who at once removed the wounded man to the hospital for medical care. These several incidents, the evidence plainly shows, created a general feeling of dislike against Corporal Fiedler. The inhabitants of Malolos apparently did not appreciate the benefits following from well-policed yards and healthful surroundings, and the accused and his followers feared and disliked the decedent because of his efficient interference with their secret incursions into Malolos. The wounding of one of these emissaries, as stated, appears to have led to a final determination on the part of the insurgents to kill Corporal Fiedler.*"[154]

Two men were given the task, allegedly at the written order of General Torres. Mariano Cruz and Marcelino Trapiel, natives of barrio San Vicente, ambushed Fiedler about 2:00 p.m. on 29 September 1900. They "waylaid" him, then Trapiel stabbed him with a dagger and Cruz shot him with a pistol. Both men were eventually identified and captured. They testified they were following "the orders of their chiefs" and were promised a reward if they succeeded. The "orders" defense carried no weight because the "accused were free to refuse to act the part of paid assassins". They were sentenced to death by hanging. Prior their execution,

---

[154] Ibid, p. 1304 and p1374; McRae was President and Rees was judge advocate in the trial of Cruz and Trapiel; Brigadier General W.H. Bisbee was President of the Court and Third Infantry 2nd Lt Robert I. Reeves was judge advocate in the Torres trial.

the two men testified at the murder trial of Torres who was charged with "murder in violation of the laws of war."

Torres was also found guilty and sentenced to death by hanging. The Commanding General's review found the two witnesses (Cruz and Trapiel) had a motive for pinning the responsibility of the murder on Torres. Further the prosecution could produce no written order signed by Torres. After review, the U.S. commanding general was:

> "*reluctant to record his conviction upon the evidence in the case, that a man of the intelligence and high command of the accused could have descended to such a cowardly act as the employment of ununiformed men to steal within the lines of his enemy to assassinate an individual soldier, merely because such enemy soldier was efficient in the performance of his bounded duty; such an act would render the author infamous in the eyes of all manly men, and cast him out from the protection the laws of war extend to honorable combatants. Upon the face of the record, the finding and sentence of the commission is justified; but for reasons stated, the commanding general of the division is pleased to give the accused the benefit of a doubt the evidence does not satisfactorily remove from his mind. The sentence is disapproved*".

Torres was set free.[155]

---

[155] **Ibid, p1304 and p1374**

Appendix 1

Infantry Regiment Composition
May 26, 1898

Adjutant General Officer General Order No. 55, May 26, 1898 outlined the infantry regiment composition in preparation for the Spanish-American War. The table called for:

1x Colonel
1x Lieutenant Colonel
2x Majors
12x Captains
14x 1st Lieutenants[156]
12x 2nd Lieutenants
1x Surgeon   2x Assistant Surgeons   3x Hospital Stewards
1 Quartermaster Sergeant
1x Chaplain
1x Regimental Sergeant Major
3x Battalion Sergeants Major
1x Chief Musician 2x Principal Musicians
2x Color Sergeants
1x Commissary Sergeant

12x Companies of Infantry organized into three battalions.

Each Company Consisted of:
1x Captain	1x 1st Lieutenant	1x 2nd Lieutenant
1x 1st Sgt	1x Quartermaster Sergeant	
4x Sergeants	8x Corporals	2x Musicians

1x Artificer
1x Wagoner
64x Privates

---

[156] **One First Lieutenant for each company for a total of 12. The two additional First Lieutenants served as Adjutant and Quartermaster, respectively.**

Infantry Regiment Composition
February 06, 1901

Consistent with the Army Reorganization Act of February 2, 1901, individual regiments were restructured by General Order No. 9, on February 6, 1901 to reflect the following:

1x Colonel
1x Lieutenant Colonel
3x Majors
15x Captains
15x 1st Lieutenants
15x 2nd Lieutenants
1x Regimental Sergeant Major
3x Battalion Sergeants Major
2x Color Sergeants
1x Quartermaster Sergeant
1x Commissary Sergeant

One Band

12x Companies of Infantry organized into three battalions of four companies each.

Each Company Consisted of:
1x Captain	1x 1st Lieutenant	1x 2nd Lieutenant
1x 1st Sergeant	1x Quartermaster Sergeant	
4x Sergeants	6x Corporals	2x Musicians
1x Artificer		
2x Cooks		
48x Privates		

The primary unit changes reflected an elimination of the medical requirements and the Chaplain, a restructuring of company grade officer requirements and the elimination of 16 infantry privates from the table of organization of each company or 192 privates at the Regimental level.

Appendix 2

Third Infantry Regiment Campaign and Service Streamers

During the Philippine Insurrection 1899-1902

Malolos Campaign
(24 March to 16 August 1899)

San Isidro Campaign
(21 April-30 May 1899)

Luzon 1899
(31 May 1899-31 Dec 1899)

Luzon 1900
(1 January 1900-31 December 1900)

No streamer was awarded for war service occurring in 1901. The Third Infantry Regiment was later mobilized for the Moro Uprising and was awarded a campaign streamer for Jolo in 1911.

Philippine war veterans were later authorized a campaign medal recognizing services from 1899 to 1913. The Army and Navy versions had slight design differences. The Army's version was authorized by the War Department General Order No. 5 on 12 January 1905.

Appendix 3
Combat Chronology
Identifiable combat actions & significant combat patrols
Third Infantry Regiment (The Old Guard)
Philippine Insurrection (1899-1902)

Date	Place	Companies Engaged	Event
Malolos Campaign *(24 March - 16 August 1899)*			
25 Mar	Caloocan	E, F, G, M (2d Bn)	Battle; Charged enemy trenches; on firing line; 20 casualties
30-Mar	Near Malolos	3d Battalion	Skirmish; Under fire of advance posts of enemy; no casualties
30-Mar	Near Malolos	B	Action; 1x WIA Co. B; on night outpost[157]
31-Mar	Malolos	3rd Infantry Regiment	Battle; 1x Officer/3x EM WIA
April 1-5	Caloocan	3rd Inf Regt	Trenches; From Caloocan to LaLoma Church
April 5-30	Malobon	B,D	Outpost; Guarding property & protecting the town
April 5-30	Caloocan	I	Outpost; Guarding roads to Manila
April 5-30	Caloocan	E	Outpost; Guarding roads & causeway to Malobon
San Isidro Campaign *(21 April - 30 May 1899)*			
22-Apr	Novaliches	A, C, F, G, H, K, L, M	
29-Apr	San Rogue	A, C, F, G, H, K, L, M	Battle; Engaged enemy for 1 hour; 2x WIA

---

[157] Abbreviation key: **WIA** = Wounded in Action; **KIA** = Killed in Action; **DOW** = Died of Wounds; **EM** = Enlisted Man; **Det**=Detachment; **Bn** = battalion; **Hq**=Headquarters; **AGO**=Adjutant Generals Office; **Arty** = Artillery; **Inf**= Infantry; **RIF**= Recon in Force.

Date	Location	Units	Notes
29-Apr	San Rafael	A, C, F, G, H, K, L, M	
1-May	San Rafael	A, C, F, G, H, K, L, M	
1-May	Near Baliuag	A, C, F, G, H, K, L, M	Battle; Engage enemy, occupy town; 2xWIA
2-May	Baliuag	A, C, F, G, H, K, L, M	
4-May	Maasin	A, C, F, G, H, K, L, M	
17-May	San Isidro	A, C, F, G, H, K, L, M	
23-May	San Ildefenso	A, C, F, G, H, K, L, M	Battle; 0745-0945; en route Baliuag; enemy repulsed; 2xWIA
23-May	Maasin	A, C, F, G, H, K, L, M	Battle; @ Noon-1 p.m.; enemy driven from positions; 3xWIA
23-May	Near Maasin	A, C, F, G, H, K, L, M	Battle; 5pm-7pm; 2 miles from Maasin; enemy \repulsed
May	Malabon	B,D	Outpost; Guarding property & protecting the town
26-May	Near Baliuag	B,D	Battle; @6pm attacked on recce; 4.miles from Baliuag; held positions for two hours when reinforcements arrived and enemy withdrew; 1xKIA
29-May	Guiguinto	B,D	Outpost; B,D rejoin Hq Company & Regimental Band
Luzon Operations (31 May - 31 December 1899)			
June	Baliuag	3d (-B,D&E)	Outpost; Regt guards trains, recon, escort wagons from Malolos
June	Guiguinto	B,D,E	Outpost
July			Same as June returns
Aug 1-12			Same as June/July Returns
13-Aug	Near Balitong	B	Action; 1Lt Arthur Edwards & 6EM on scout/fired on; 1xWIA
13-Aug	Near Bintong	3d Infantry Regiment	Battle; Col. Page leads recon in force with 3d Inf, Troop K of 4th

Date	Location	Unit	Notes
			Cavalry, and one section of Battery G, 3d Arty on Guiguinto Road to attack. "The command under Col. Page struck the enemy near Bintong and routed them after an engagement of one hour. B, D return to Guiguinto and remainder of force return to Baluag; 1xKIA. 2xEM drown while crossing the Bag Bag River.
14-Aug	near Guiguinto	C, E, F, G	
14-Aug	Baliuag	L	Action; Outpost fired on; return fire; no casualties
15-Aug	to Pulilan	H, M	Recce; Recon-in-force; no casualties
15-Aug	to San Rafael	L	Recce; w/Troop K, 4th Cavalry; no casualties
4 Sept	to Pulilan	2nd Battalion	Recce; (E, F, G, M) under Capt. L.W. Cooke; 20 miles; 0245-0600 hrs
6 Sept	to San Rafael	A, G, I, K, L	Recce; Capt. W.C. Brettler leads; no resistance encountered but 10 POWs captured; 5 rifles & 300 rounds ammo; 12 miles
1-Oct	---	---	Regt organized into Battalions to comply with AGO orders
1-Oct	San Fernando	1st Battalion	On Duty; Unit moves from Baliuag to Malolos; via rail to San Fernando
1 Oct	Baliuag	3d Battalion	On Duty
Oct.	Guingua	B, D	Outpost; Ft. Stotsenberg
7 Oct	Guingua	B, D	Action; Outpost fired on; no casualties
12 Oct	Guingua	B, D	Action; Outpost fired on; no casualties
13 Oct	Guingua	B, D	Action; Outpost fired on; no casualties

Date	Location	Unit	Description
14 Oct	Guingua	B, D	Action; Outpost fired on; no casualties
14/15 Oct	Baliuag	6 Companies	Action; 6 companies of 3rd Inf, one troop of 4th Cavalry and two pieces of artillery; Outposts on east, north and west flank attacked at 9:30 pm, 11:30 pm and 1:30 am; Estimate 2000 insurgents and four field guns in area; Siege anticipated but did not develop.
22 Oct	Guingua	D	Action; Capt Sample and 40 men captured 12 bandits and rescue one Chinese merchant; one bandit KIA
23 Oct	Guingua	B,D	Action; 30 man patrol, native scout and Chinese merchant for decoy captured 10 additional bandits northwest of town.
23 Oct	Bulacan	B	Action; 25 guerillas launch night attack on outpost; US Private Robert McNave WIA through accidental explosion of cartridge.
25 Oct		Det, 3rd Inf	Raid
28 Oct	Lugan	Det, 3rd Inf	Raid; 80 troops; the two actions of 25 and 28 Oct resulted in the destruction of insurgent buildings, 12 POWs, one Remington rifle and ammunition.
9-Nov	to Luboa	E, F	Action; Capt McRae conducts recon;" Encountered small outpost of insurgents"; no casualties
24-Nov	Florida Blanca	2nd Battalion	Recce to Florida Blanca and Porac; Capt McRae leads 2nd Bn; nothing to report
24 Nov	Maasin	I, K, L	Battle; w/Battery G, 3d Arty; RIF; "Encountered enemy in force and drove them from their positions"

24 Nov	San Ildefonso	I, K, L	Battle; w/ Battery G; RIF; Battled one hour; "drove enemy out of strong positions. 2Lt Maxwell Keyes, Co. L, killed while leading scouts"; Pvt Stone, Co. A, KIA
3-Dec	Expedition	A, B, C	**Units join 16th Infantry on 12/4; to San Miquel**
4 Dec	San Ildefonso	A, B, C	Skirmish (near here)
6 Dec	Maasin	A, B, C	Action
8 Dec	Baliuag	A, B, C	Return to Post
4 Dec	San Ildefonso	Co. I, K, L	
10-Dec	San Ildenfenso	A, B, C/Regt	Battle; Regiment strikes enemy at San Ildefenso; no casualties
15-Dec	Baliuag	Regt	Regt returns to Post
18-Dec	Guiguinto	Regt	Concentrates; conducts patrols, recce, scouts
19 Dec	Caloocan	--	
4 Dec	Expedition	E, F, G, H	BG Grant leads 750-man expedition of 3rd Inf (300 men), 32nd Inf (400 men), and Battery. K, 3rd Arty (50 men) into southwestern Pampanga, Bataan and Zambales Provinces uniting with 25th Infantry on 12 December. The expedition's objective was to clear out the insurgents.
4 Dec	Dinalupijan	E, F, G, H	Action; Capt. McRae w/300 men drive force of enemy at daylight; three enemy KIA; captured 10 rifles and 2,000 rounds of ammunition.
5 Dec	Orani	E, F, G, H	Action; Capt. McRae drive force of enemy; two enemy KIA; two revolvers and six homemade cannon captured.

6 Dec	Balanga	E, F, G, H	Action; Capt. McRae drive force of enemy; two enemy KIA; three rifles, two revolvers and four "old" cannon were captured.
9 Dec	Olongapo	Det, 3rd Inf	Action: Capt McRae and 100 selected 3rd Infantrymen participated in capture of Olongapo capturing naval arsenal and quantity of stores; attacked at Iba, capturing three rifles and six pieces of old 'dismounted' artillery; two enemy KIA and two enemy WIA.
10 Dec	Subic Bay	E, H	Action; Subic Occupied. Two enemy KIA; two rifles, 200 rounds of ammo, 1200 bushels of rice, and 300 pounds of salt were captured. [158]
11 Dec	Near San Miguel	A, B, C	
11 Dec	San Ildefenso	A, B, C	
12 Dec	Castillejos	Det, 3rd Inf	Action: Capt McRae's force encounters insurgents killing two; 25 prisoners rescued (Filipino and Spanish)
14 Dec	Near Olongapo	Det 32nd and 3rd Infantry	Action: Capt Sevier, 32nd Inf engage enemy with one enemy KIA "on whom was found a U.S. haversack". Destroyed enemy blockhouse and stockade "formerly used as a signal station by the enemy".
14 Dec	Near Aglau	Det 3rd Inf	Action: Capt McRae, one enemy KIA and one enemy WIA; captured 2 carabaos, a cart load of insurgent clothing and two ponies.

---

[158] **About 200 men of the McRae's Third Infantry Detachment, a platoon of artillery, and many of the sick were detached to return to Florida Blanca before the Olongapo skirmish.**

18 Dec	Mariveles	Det 3rd Inf	Action: Capt McRae's Det- attacked at daylight capturing three rifles and one insurgent WIA.
Luzon Operations (1900)			
2/3 Jan	Near Florida Blanca	Detachment, 3rd Inf	Action: Lt Burr and Lt Rees and 20 men of 3rd Inf at Florida Blanca acting on tip that 50 insurgents were in San Pedro, launched raid. Captured an insurgent Lieutenant who revealed 22 Remington rifles, one Japanese rifle, one Krag, 26 cartridge belts and 1,000 rounds of ammunition. Returned to base by 0750 am.
3 Jan	San Pedro	F, G	Action; Capt. McRae leads scout; captures 24 rifles, 1000 rounds
5 Jan	Lubao	Det, 3rd Inf	Action: Capt McRae, Lt Burr with 100 men (50 each) surround town, capture insurgent sergeant and 14 privates.
Jan 7-26	San Jose	F,G	Scout; Captain James H. McRae leads 19-day, 280 mile expedition "for the purpose of cleaning up the adjacent country and clearing it of insurgents." Departs San Jose on Jan. 7, 1900; also had 49 Macabebe scouts and 30 mounted men among his 6 officers and 145 men from Companies F and G; captured Mauser and ammunition, one insurgent officer and 25 enlisted prisoners (the latter were released).
8 Jan	Near Atlog	Det, 3rd Inf	Action; 2Lt Dockery and 1Lt Ross with 71 Macabebe scouts engage about 40 insurgents at noon; "scouts returned fire and charged the enemy, who

			immediately gave way and scattered in the swamps"; found a barracks with armracks. Destroyed 1,000 rounds of Remington ammunition.
9 Jan	Quila	F, G	Action; Captured five rifles, 200 rounds ammo.
9 Jan	Santa Rita	Det, 3rd Inf	Action: Lt Burr with 16 men kill three, wound ten enemy and capture two rifles.
10 Jan	Near Pulilan	H	Lt Houle and one platoon of Co. H conduct scout.
10 Jan	Santa Tomas	Scout, 3rd	Action: Comandante Perfecto captured during routine scout.
10 Jan	Near Baboulaz	Det, 3rd Infantry	Action; AGO Records-no officer identified; no details
11 Jan	Pulanlay	F, G	Skirmish; No casualties; two rifles captured
11 Jan	Quingua	I	Capt Freeland and one platoon of Co. I conduct scout in direction of Quingua; nothing unusual to report.
12 Jan	Florida Blanca	F, G	Action; Insurgents surrender 35 rifles
17 Jan	Banibaug	Det. 3d Infantry	Action; McRae-AGO Records, no details; possibly Banaba where one insurgent and one insurgent leader's (Mascardo) horse was captured; at Palisapi liberated one Spanish prisoner and captured two insurgent officers.
17 Jan	Near Malolos	Det., 3d Infantry	Action; AGO Records-Lt Houle; no details
17 Jan	Calang	Det., 3d Infantry	Action; McRae-AGO Records, no details; Grant reported Calang (near Dumandan) was occupied by Gen. Hizon and 400 men – 25 present when McRae arrived to capture ten POWs, four storehouses with several tons of rice and a barracks. Barracks and rice were burned.

18 Jan	Dumandan near Mabalacat	Det., 3d Infantry	Battle of Lumandan; McRae-AGO Records, no details; Grant reports Gen. Hizon and 50 insurgents engaged McRae's force. McRae said Filipino forces "made stubborn resistance. Detachment gallantly charged up steep bank and captured entrenchments. Position inaccessible from this side of mountains, except one place where only few could go up at a time, so steep that men had to assist each other up bank. Insurgents held trench and continued to fire until we were within a few yards then fled back into the mountains. Gen. Hizon fled into the mountains in direction of Zambales when alarm first given by fire of outpost. Four insurgents and first lieutenant killed in trenches and buried. Informed by captured officer that Lt Col Rivera was also killed but carried away; number of wounded unknown. We had one man wounded in hand, one captain and one soldier taken prisoners. Two United States Government mules, about 130 rifles, and several rounds ammunition captured. Factory for reloading ammunition, which also contained quantity of rice, destroyed."
18 Jan	Near Porac	Det., 3rd Infantry	Action; McRae-AGO Records, no details
19 Jan	Polo	E?	Action: Grant reports a Private Badford was captured by two

			armed insurgents on road to barrio Alando "and confined him to a house to the left of that barrio, where insurgents decided to take him to swamps between there and Malabon. Badford escaped, reporting facts to Lt. Stewart, who took squad and endeavored to capture insurgents. Badford reported to have seen two insurgents with arms and 10 bolos. Lt. Stewart captured one man identified by Badford as one of the insurgents who stood guard over him. No other capture was made."
19 Jan	Banola	F, G	Action; Captured important papers of Gen. Mascardo
21 Jan	Banola	F, G	Action; Insurgents surrender 35 rifles; possibly Lt. Burr's event (with mounted detachment) where 36 rifles were purchased at 30 pesos each; also captured one insurgent captain, one lieutenant and one soldier. Reported by Grant.
24 Jan	West of Banaba	Det, 3rd Inf	Action: Capt McRae reports capture of 10 bull-cart loads of powder and ammunition stored in mountains west of Banaba; Magazine and three other buildings used as barracks burned.
24 Jan	Parado	Det, 3rd Inf	Action: Lt. Moore makes scout and captures three POWs and three rifles.
25 Jan	Near Banola	F, G	Action; Insurgent powder factory captured; 1.5 tons of powder; 200 large gun (arty) projectiles and powder making equipment
26 Jan	San Jose	F, G	Return to Base; Capt. McRae's scout returns to base having

Date	Location	Unit	Description
			killed five insurgents, taken three prisoners of war, captured 273 rifles, 200 artillery rounds and over 1700 rounds of small arms ammo
28 Jan	Santa Cruz	Det, 3rd Inf	Action: Scouting party from Capt McRae's command surprised Lt Col Hizon's soldiers in a house at Santa Cruz near Baraurya. Hizon and one insurgent soldier badly wounded.
28 Jan	Lampoc Mountain	G	Action: Lt Rees captures 1,000 rounds of ammunition near mountain.
28 Jan	Near Lalintoque	F	Action: Lt. Barker on scout fired upon by insurgents. "Returned fire with vigor and saw about 30 insurgents retreat over hills"; scouted trail in neighboring ravine and was fired upon by two Negritos at a distance of 500 yards; found military quarters at head of ravine, which were burned."
29 Jan	Near Pulilan	I	Action: Capt Freeland, Lt Ross with Co. I, 3rd Inf, and Lt. O'Connell with 16 Macabebe Scouts; fired on near Pulilan.
4 Feb	Malolos	F	Co F left San Jose, marched to San Fernando and then by rail to Malolos, taking station there.
7 Feb	Manila	B	Event: According to the Report of the Philippine Commission (p486), Report of the Philippine Commission, Appendix W, Report of the Auditor to the Secretary of Finance and Justice), Captain Arthur Williams, 3rd Inf, Malabon, made a Special Deposit (No. 27) on 7 February 1900 for the sum of $322 Mexican funds. The

			money was reported to be insurgent funds and to have been taken from two natives in August 1899. The money could be from 13 Aug 1899 event.
8 Feb		Scout, 3rd Inf	Action: "A scouting party of the Third Infantry succeeded in capturing Cipriano Paschecho, known as "general", though his real rank appears to be colonel in the insurgent army. He was sent to Manila pursuant to telegraphic instructions dated February 8. When captured he had 470 pesos in his possession and horse and saddle."
9 Feb		Det, 3rd Inf	Action: capture two lists of soldiers in the insurgent army and two letters relating to contributions. The body of Harry Dunlap, 3rd Infantry, was founded and disinterred by a party from Bulacan.
13 Feb	Navotas	B	Action: Lt. McDaniel and 11 men arrested four natives, "the principal one being Simon Blas, who had a Remington in his house and a large sum of money – 500 pesos in coin and deposit receipts for 900 pesos. Blas claimed to have gotten the money by trading, but examination of papers found in his house point to his connection with Paschecho, Montenegros, and other insurrectos. Leon Santos, a relative of Blas has also about 1,000 pesos in coin".
24 Feb	Navotas	Det, 3rd Inf	Action: Lt Wygant with 8 men of company, band, interpreter, and native guide disguised, left Malabon and proceeding to the island of Navotas, across the

Date	Location		Description
			river, reached the house of Presidente Silvester Pascual. This placed was surrounded, and also the house of his clerk, Justo Pas. Among the papers founded were communications addressed to the president, lists of cabezas, and police in Navotas, and a receipt for three Remington and one Mauser Americano, dated Manila, February 22, given to Pascual."
3 Mar	Iba	H	Lt Dockery and 20 men reconnoitered from Hagonoy to barrio of Iba; captured one Remington rifle and cartridge pouch, a quantity of rice, provisions and furniture.
18-Mar	Polumgubat	L	Action; AGO Records-no officer named; possibly effort to arrest Innocentcio Tolentine, insurrecto governor of Guiguinto by Capt Nichols. Captured one rifle, one pouch of ammunition, a hat, and three insurrectos. [Editor's Note: Tolentine may be Aurelio Tolentino, 1867-1915, a famous Filipino playwright and insurgent leader.]
19 Mar		L	Action: Capt Nichols repots capture of three POWs, one Mauser rifle and one pouch of Mauser ammo. (May be event of 18th)
22-Mar	Novaliches	E	Action; Capt. McRae left Meycauayan at 0330 & marched to barrio of Ugong; no resistance; captured 64 rifles, 2000 rounds small arms ammo & 19 POWs; marched 12 miles
April	Hagonoy	I	Scout, Capt Freeland and scouting parting capture four guns and one revolver.

Date	Location	Co.	Description
3-Apr	Near Apalit	K	Action; AGO Records; no details; Wheaton reports "Lt Burr's scouts captured one rifle and killed one ladrones near Florida Blanca."
6-Apr	San Rosario	--	Patrol, captured two shotguns, one Mauser and one Remington.
10-Apr	San Isabela	I	Scout, Lt. Smith and 23 men, captured one Mauser, one Remington and 17 rounds of ammunition.
4-Jun	Barrio Louca	G	Battle; Co. G was attached to 35th Inf; at Barrio Louca encountered and routed insurgents; no casualties.
7-Jun	Balibag	G, H	Scout; Proceeded against insurgent stronghold at Balibag; no resistance reported.
11-Jun	Balubad	E, F, G	Action; Expedition with detachments of 4th Cavalry, 3rd Inf, 35th Inf, 41st Inf, district scouts and Light Battery E, 1st Arty, attacked the camp of the insurgents at Mount Balubad near Biacnabato, which was captured and destroyed. Inflicted heavy loss. US loss was one WIA.
20 Jun	Porac	Det, 3rd Inf	Action; Lt Giddings in command of mounted scouts, 3rd Inf, captured 13 rifles and 1,000 rounds of ammunition.
2-Jul	Gotung	H	Action; AGO records; Sgt Merriam event (see below).
3-Jul	Tibaguin	H	Battle; Sgt Merriam and Detachment of 20 men in search of the robbers of the steamboat 'Filipino' are ambushed while traveling in bancas; They immediately landed and routed the enemy inflicting 12 KIA, 14 WIA, capturing 12 rifles. Reinforcements under Lt. John

Date	Location	Unit	Event
			H. Page, Jr. arrive about 10:30 a.m. and drive off enemy; 3 US KIA and 2 US WIA; Corporal Frank Wallace nominated for CMOH.
4 Jul	Paombong	Det, 3rd Inf	Action; Lt Rees and detachment scouting near Malolos in bancas on the Santa Cruz River; fired on by enemy from the bank; detachment lands and drives off the enemy capturing one rifle and 200 rounds of ammunition; One US KIA and three WIA.
8 Jul	Ubiajn	E	Action; Capt McRae, struck ladrones; captured three or four rifles and 195 rounds of ammunition. No casualties.
27-Jul	Polo	E	Action; Detachment fired upon; no casualties
16-Sep	Polo	E	Battle; 125 insurgents attack 16 man outpost (two corporals and 14 privates); enemy driven off; no U.S. casualties
16 Sep	Guiguinto	G	Battle; Platoon under 1Lt H.A. Smith attacked by 300 insurgents; one hour battle; 2 US WIA
20-Sep	Atlog	L, F	Action; 2Lt George Lewis with 21 men of Co. L and 16 men of Co. F capture insurgent arsenal hidden in swamp; three enemy KIA, 9 POWs, capture nine small banca boats, gold specie, 1000 pounds of rice, 100 pounds of sheet brass, 3000 rounds of ammunition, seven rifles and a quantity of rifle parts and powder taken. Burned arsenal and 11 other buildings including Torre's headquarters and personal effects to include papers. One man wounded.

Date	Location	Unit	Description
20-Sep	Malolos		Action-AGO records; may be Ailag Raid; no details.
23 Sep	Marilao Bridge	Det, 3rd Inf	Action: Detachment attacked by insurgents around 9:30 pm. No casualties.
23 Sept	Bahari-Pari	E	Action: Capt McRae and 25 men surprised insurgents and captured 26 in the cuartel (barracks), 22 Remingtons, 300 rounds of ammunition. Two insurgent WIA attempting to escape.
4 Oct	La Lomboy	A	Scout, Lt Sharp and detachment capture three Ladrones, two rifles, destroyed Cuartel and 8000 pounds of rice. No casualties.
10 Oct	Near Atlog	2nd Battalion	Lt Moore and 50 men proceeded down Calanata River and attacked insurgent revenue-collecting station one mile below Atlog. Two insurgent KIA, one WIA and one revolver and papers captured.
24 Oct	Avon	Det, 3rd Inf	Lt Humphrey and 12 mounted men attack 18 insurgents near barrio and killed nine. They were waiting to ambush General Grant. U.S. was tipped off. Lt. Humphrey responded. No casualties.
24 Nov	Near Malolos	F, L	Action; On patrol; Lt Lewis and 39 men fired on with one volley from ambush; 1 US KIA and 2 US WIA.
30 Nov to 1 Dec	Malolos	Det, 3rd Inf	Expedition; Column consisting of 5th District Scouts, 41st Inf Scouts, Macabebe Scouts and detachment of 3rd Infantry thoroughly scout swamps south of Malolos to clear district of

				insurgents and ladrones.
Dec. 9	La Lomboy	H, E		Battle
Luzon Operations (1901)				
13 Feb	Hagonoy	I		Event; Operations in vicinity of Hagonoy resulted in the surrender of Maximo Angeles, 112 rifles, and 1500 rounds of ammunition to Capt Freeland.
19 Feb	Malolos	3rd Inf		Major Eugenio Hernando surrenders.
23/24 Feb	Near Santa Cruz	L		Action; Lt Lewis, while scouting nipa swamps near Calanata River came into contact with armed insurgents or ladrones three times on the 23rd and twice on the 24th. Killed Amolate Alonzo, captain of guerillas, captured two rifles and 275 rounds of ammunition. No U.S. casualties.
3 Mar	Bigaa	A		Action; Sgt Reynolds had fight with insurgents north of Bigaa; captured four insurgents of Biloz's band and one rifle.
3 Mar	Looc	L		Action; Capt Kilbourne with detachment of native scouts from Malolos, struck band of six insurgents while searching for rifles; killed three insurgents including Capt Jacob Santos, the commander.
16 Mar	--	M		Action; Lt Gibson, while scouting with four mounted men, encountered 10 insurgents under Biloz. Gibson attacked and gave chase capturing four men, three rifles and a revolver.
19 Mar	Near Presna	E		Action; Capt McRae and 35 men discovered 25 armed insurgents on the south bank of Marilao River; two insurgent KIA; one

Date	Location	Unit	Event
			officer WIA and made POW with additional enlisted POW; two rifles and 50 rounds of ammunition captured. Supposed to have been troops under Morales.
25 Mar	Apalit	Capt Butler	Lt Col Donato Fedora surrenders with four weapons.
25 Mar	Near Atlog	L	Action; Lt Lewis and eight native scouts on patrol in swamps attacked and fired on; two Ladrones KIA.
1 Apr	Malabon	3rd Inf	Teodoro Gonzales surrenders with 12 officers, 44 men and 4 weapons.
18-Apr	Angat	G, F[159]	Scout; Capt. McRae leads a mounted detachment on scout; depart at 0530 for mountains east of Norzagary to punish General Torres' insurgents force
18-Apr	Near Norzagary	G, F	Action; One insurgent KIA and several POWs, two rifles captured
19-Apr	Near Norzagary	G, F	Action; Three rifles captured
21-Apr	Near Norzagary	G, F	Action; Two rifles captured
22-Apr	Angat	G, F	Det returns to base about 1700; marched 79 miles. Higher HQs summary of expedition reflects three combat actions with seven enemy KIA; 20 POWs; 22 rifles and over 300 rounds of ammunition.
24 Apr	Norzagary	G,F	General Isidro Torres, with six men, surrenders to Capt. McRae.
25-	Near	G, F	Action; Captain Vaillanera

---

[159] This expedition primarily 38 men of Company G, 16 Macabebe Scouts, ten native scouts, and mounted detachment of 38 men consisting of Third Infantry and Macabebes for 102 total. Officers included 1st Lt Hamilton A. Smith, 2nd Lt Robert I Rees and 2nd Lt Frederick B. Hennessey of Twenty-Seventh Infantry.

Date	Place	Officer	Description
Apr	Norzagary		surrenders with 11 enlisted men and 12 rifles; In earlier skirmish, two insurgents KIA and 22 more rifles captured; marched 39 miles; This is the last major combat action reported in the Returns of the 3rd U.S. Infantry for 1901.
29 Apr	Norzagary	Col. Page	Captain Sisson surrenders with 27 men and 24 weapons.
17 Dec	Sampa	Lt Faulkner	Action; Lt. A.U. Faulkner with Macabebe scouts struck about 20 insurgents near Sampa, barrio of San Luis capturing one Remington rifle; no casualties. This was part of a five-day scout in mountains east of Batangas with Lt Van Voorhis with 50 native scouts, Third Cavalry and 10 men of 20th and 21st Inf. Also recovered were three unserviceable shotguns.
22 Dec	Pulunganajo	Lt Faulkner	Lt. A.U. Faulkner, Third Infantry, with 11 native scouts, Second Company of Macabebe, and native guide found three Mausers, three Remingtons, three Muratas, one Springfield rifle, and 250 rounds of ammunition. All the guns were serviceable.

Various detachments are relieved throughout 1901 by Macabebe Scouts; other outposts are abandoned as the regiment prepares for a return to U.S.

On March 12, 1902, the unit concentrates at Camp Wallace, Manila; embarks U.S. transport *Thomas* and sails for U.S. on March 17 arriving in San Francisco on April 15, 1902 after three years service.

Sources of Information: Official Returns, Third Infantry Regiment 1898-1902; AGO Records, Official Correspondence, and War Department Annual Reports to Congress.

Appendix 4 – Regimental Roster

Regimental Officers [160]
Third U.S. Infantry
In Service in the Philippine Islands 1899-1902

Name	Co	Rank
Adams, Henry H.[161]	F&S	Lt Col
Ball, William G.	1st Bn	QM and CS
Barker, John W.[162]	F	Captain/Commanding Company
Baskette, Alvin K.[163]	F	1st Lt
Bathiany, Harry W.[164]	K	2nd Lt
Beall, Fielder M.M[165].	K	Captain/Adjutant
Brown, Walter S.[166]	F	2nd Lt
Bugge[167], Jens	D	1st Lt
Burr, Frank S.[168]	Atch	1st Lt/11th Inf
Buttler, William C.[169]	K	Captain/Commanding Co

---

[160] Abbreviations: F&S=Field and Staff; Bn=Battalion; QM=Quartermaster; CS=Chief of Staff; Col= Colonel; Lt Col=Lieutenant Colonel; Maj=Major; Capt=Captain; 1st Lt = First Lieutenant; 2nd Lt= Second Lieutenant; Atch=Attached to the regiment; ADC is Aide-de-Camp; Co = Company; Div = Division; Dept=Department

[161] Adams, of Ohio, enlisted as a Private in the 98th Ohio infantry eventually achieving the rank of Colonel, 5th U.S. Infantry in 1903.

[162] Barker, of New York, USMA Class of 1890.

[163] Baskette, of Tennessee, 1st Sgt 1st Tennessee Infantry May 1898; 2nd Lt 26 Oct 1898; transferred to USV then Third Infantry.

[164] Bathiany, of Kentucky, enlisted Musician 2nd KY Infantry 6 May 1898; commissioned 2 Feb 1901.

[165] Beall, of Maryland, Private and Sergeant Signal Corps, 1870 to 1883; 2nd Lt 1883; Capt, 3d Inf, 1 Jan 1899.

[166] Brown, of Maine, USMA '95; 2nd Lt 15 Feb 1899; 1st Lt 4th Inf 20 Sept 1900; transferred to 10th Inf 18 August 1902.

[167] Bugge, of Wisconsin/Minnesota; USMA '91; 2nd Lt Third Inf June 1895; 1st Lt Jan 1899; Capt in 28th Inf 2 Feb 1901.

[168] Burr, of Nebraska, enlisted Private 2nd Nebraska Infantry 13 May 1898; 2nd Lt Third Inf July 1898; transferred to 11th Inf October 1899.

[169] Buttler, of New Jersey, USMA '72; 2nd Lt Third Inf June 1876; Major in March 1901.

Cabell, Henry C.[170]	H	Captain
Caulding, William	F&S	Major
Clark, Rufus B.[171]	L	1st Lt
Cook, William H.[172]	Atch	Surgeon/Major
Cooke, Lorenzo W.[173]	F/2nd Bn	Captain/Commanding Bn
Day, Frederick R.[174]	M	Captain/Commanding Co
Dockery, Oliver H., Jr.[175]	H	1st Lt
Driver, Gerry S.[176]	Atch	Surgeon/Capt
Dwyer, Charles G.[177]	A	Captain
Edwards, Arthur M.[178]	B	1st Lt
Faulkner, Albert U.[179]	C	2nd Lt
Freeland, Harry[180]	I	Captain/Commanding Co
Frissell, Thomas T.[181]	3rd Bn	Adjutant

[170] Cabell, of Virginia, USMA '79; Captain to Third Inf 1 Jan 1899; transferred to 14th Inf 26 Oct 1900.

[171] Clark, of Georgia, Private to QM Sgt, 1st Washington Inf, April 1898; 1st Lt to Third Inf Feb 1901.

[172] Cook, of Illinois/California, Capt 6th California Inf, April 1898; 1st Lt Surgeon 32nd USV July 1899; Major Surgeon of Volunteers, 11 March 1901; disch 25 Nov 1902.

[173] Cooke, of New York, Private/Corporal 27th Wisconsin Infantry, July 1862; 2nd Lt Third Inf September 1866; Major 26th Inf Feb 1901.

[174] Day, of New York, Private and Sergeant Signal Corps, 6 August 1880; 2nd Lt 1884; Captain Third Inf January 1899.

[175] Dockery, of North Carolina, 2nd Lt 1st NC Inf Nov 1898; to Third Inf April 1899; 1st Lt Feb 1901.

[176] Driver, of D.C. Captain and Assistant Surgeon of Volunteers, Feb 1901; hon disch Feb 1903.

[177] Dwyer, of Texas, USMA '86; Major to Colonel of 1st Texas Infantry; mustered out of Volunteers 18 April 1899; appointed Captain Third Inf March 1899.

[178] Edwards, of New York and Nebraska; USMA '93; 1st Lt Third Inf April 1898; transferred to 14th Inf 11 Oct 1899/

[179] Faulkner, of New York, Private NY Cavalry June 1898; 2nd Lt USV July 1899; 2nd Lt Third Inf Feb 1901; transfer to Artillery Corps March 1902.

[180] Freeland, of Maryland, USMA '86; Captain Third Inf March 1899; retired 21 Oct 1902.

[181] Frissell, of Missouri, USMA '97; 1st Lt Third Inf March 1899; Captain, 5th Inf April 1902.

Gibson, William R.[182]	M	1st Lt
Giddings, Paul[183]	D	1st Lt
Goodale, Greenleaf A.[184]	F&S	Lt Col
Hagsdall, Ralph	A	1st Lt
Hannay, John W.[185]	F&S	Major
Hart, Patrick J.[186]	Atch	Chaplain
Houle, George E.[187]	H	1st Lt/Commanding Co.
Huck, George E.	H	1st Lt/Commanding Co.
Humphrey, Chauncey B.[188]	E/5th Dist Staff	1st Lt/Engineer Officer
Hurst, Paul[189]	D/1st Bn	Adjutant
Jackson, William P.[190]	F&S	Quartermaster
Jones, Charles Carlton[191]	I	2nd Lt
Keller, Charles[192]	M	2nd Lt

---

[182] Gibson, of Ohio and Iowa, Captain 51st Iowa Inf April 1898; 2nd Lt Third Inf June 1899; 1st Lt Feb 1901.

[183] Giddings, of Minnesota; Army enlisted from Private to 1st Sgt, 8th Cavalry, 1892-1897; 2nd Lt Third Inf March 1897; 1st Lt March 1899; Captain, 17th Inf Nov 1901; transferred back to Third Inf May 1902.

[184] Goodale, of Maine, Private through Sergeant, 6th Maine Infantry in Civil War, May 1861-Jan 1864; 1st Lt 77th U.S. C Inf, Jan 1864; Brevet Major of Vols, March 1865; mustered out Nov 1866; 1st Lt 2Third Infantry July 1866; Captain June 1878; Major April 1898; Lt Col Third Inf July 1899; Colonel 17th Inf April 1901; Brigadier General 23 Feb 1903; retired 24 Feb 1903.

[185] Hannay, of England and Pennsylvania; Civil War veteran, 1st Lt 198th Pa and 1st US Inf (64-65); 2nd Lt Third Inf 1866; thru Major in March 1899; Lt Col 12th Inf, July 1901; retired October 1901.

[186] Hart, of Ohio/Minnesota; Chaplain Feb 1893; 8th Inf Feb 1901 and 13th Cavalry August 1901.

[187] Houle, Canada and Massachusetts, USMA '93; to Third Inf; Captain 26th Inf Feb 1901.

[188] Humphrey, of Kansas, USMA '98, 2nd Lt to Third Inf; 1st Lt March 1899; transferred to 17th Inf 7 Feb 1903; Captain of 22nd Inf 10 Feb 1903.

[189] Hurst, of NJ and DC, 2nd Lt Third Inf April 1899; 1st Lt Feb 1901.

[190] Jackson, of Missouri, USMA '91; Captain Third Inf November 1900.

[191] Jones, of Iowa, Sgt 51st Iowa Volunteer Inf April 1898; 2nd Lt 11th Vol Cav July 1900; 2nd Lt Third Inf Feb 1901.

[192] Keller, of Idaho and Texas, 2nd Lt Third Inf Feb 1901.

Kilbourne, Lincoln F.[193]	L	1st Lt
Langdon, Russell C.[194]	M	1st Lt
Lewis, George C.[195]	L	2nd Lt
McAndrew, James W.[196]	F&S	QM/Captain
McArthur, John C.[197]	A	1st Lt
McCall, James H.[198]	Atch	Surgeon/Capt
McCoy, Frank B.[199]	C/G	Captain
McDaniel, Wilbur A.[200]	B	2nd Lt
McGonnigle, George A.	F&S	Major
McPherson, William E.[201]	Atch	Surgeon/Capt
McRae, James H.[202]	E	Captain/Commanding
Mitchell, Henry T.	Atch	2nd Lt/41st Inf
Moore, James T.[203]	2nd Bn	Adjutant

[193] Kilbourne, of California and Ohio, USMA '93; Third Inf May 1899; Capt 26th Inf Feb 1901.
[194] Langdon, of NY, USMA '96; 1st Lt Third Inf August 1899; Capt, 9th Inf July 1901; tr back to Third Inf June 1902.
[195] Lewis, of Missouri, Private/Corporal, 1st USV Inf June 1898; Sgt Third Cav Dec 1898; 2nd Lt Third Inf July 1900.
[196] McAndrew, of Pennsylvania, USMA '88; 1st Lt Third Inf May 1895; Captain March 1899.
[197] McArthur, of Minnesota and South Dakota, USMA '94; 1st Lt Third Inf April 1898; transferred to 28th Inf Dec 1899; Capt Feb 1901.
[198] McCall, of Tennessee, Capt and Assistant Surgeon of Volunteers, Feb 1901; disch 31 Dec 1901.
[199] McCoy, of Georgia and Missouri; 2nd Lt Third Inf Feb 1883; 1st Lt 1887; Lt Col 12th Minnesota Volunteer Infantry May 1898; Captain, Regulars, Third Inf 15 Nov 1899.
[200] McDaniel, of Ohio, Private and Corporal, 6th Inf April 1897; 2nd Lt Third Inf October 1899; 1st Lt May 1901.
[201] McPherson, of Massachusetts; Hospital Steward 5th Mass Inf June 1898; 1st Lt Asst Surgeon Oct 1898; Captain, Asst Surgeon, USV, March 1901; disch Feb 1903.
[202] McRae, of Georgia, USMA '86; to Third Inf 1886; 1st Lt 14th Inf Oct 1892; transferred back to Third Inf Dec 1892; Captain in March 1899; cited for gallantry in Cuba (Silver Star equivalent) and later in Philippines; Major General commanding 78th Infantry Division in World War I.
[203] Moore, of Connecticut and Michigan, USMA '92; Third Inf June 1892; 1st Lt April 1898; Captain 27th Inf Feb 1901.

Nichols, Maury[204]	L	Captain/Commanding Co
Noble, Robert H.[205]	B/Dept of Visayas	Captain/Adjt Gen Dept
Orchard, Samuel C.[206]	A	2nd Lt
Page, John H.[207]	F&S	Colonel
Page, John H., Jr.[208]	I/3rd Bn	2Lt/QM and CS/Co. I
Pitcher, George S.	F&S	Acting Assistant Surgeon
Plummer, William H.[209]	E	2nd Lt
Pond, George B.[210]	K	1st Lt

---

[204] Nichols, DC and NY; 2nd Lt 16th Inf 1883; Captain, Third Inf Jan 1899.
[205] Noble, of Maryland, USMA '84; 2nd Lt 1st Inf; Major AAG to Volunteers June 1898; Captain (Regulars) October 1898; assigned Third Inf Jan 1899.
[206] Orchard, of Texas, 1st Lt Texas Vol Infantry, April 1898; 2nd Lt (Regular) Third Inf Feb 1901.
[207] Page was born 26 March 1842 New Castle, Delaware. He was the son of Captain John Page who was killed in the battle of Palo Alto in the Mexican War; Civil War veteran; Private, 1st Illinois Light Arty Aug to Oct '61; 2nd Lt Third US Inf August '61; Captain, May 1864; Major, 11th Inf Sept 1885; Lt Col, 22nd Inf Feb 1891; Colonel, Third Inf May 1895; Brigadier General of Volunteers, 21 Sept 1898; hon disc from Vols 30 Nov 1898; brevet to Captain 13 Dec 1862 for gallantry and meritorious service in the battle of Fredericksburg, Va and brevet for Major 2 July 1863 for gallantry and meritorious service at Gettysburg. He was retired at his request on 27 July 1903 after 40 years service. He was one of 34 Civil War veterans and Colonels promoted to the rank of Brigadier General one day before retirement at the direction of the President. He died, age 75, at West Point, NY at the home of his daughter 9 October 1916 and is buried at Arlington National Cemetery, Section E, D S Site 1286.; see *San Francisco Chronicle*, 18 July 1903, p2, 'Promotion for Army Officers'.
[208] Page, Jr., born 10 Jan 1875 in Louisiana; 2nd Lt Third Inf Sept 1899; 1st Lt 6th Inf March 1901; Lt Col of 61st Infantry at time of retirement. He died 25 April 1959. Buried at Section 2, Site 1227 RH, Arlington National Cemetery.
[209] Plummer of Rhode Island and Mass; 2nd Lt 2nd Mass Inf May 1898; 2nd Lt (Regulars) Third Inf Feb 1901; 1st Lt 6th Inf April 1902.
[210] Pond, of North Carolina; 2nd Lt Third Inf Sept 1898; 1st Lt 4th Inf Oct 1899; trans back to Third Inf May 1900.

Potter, Samuel O.L.[211]	Atch	Surgeon
Rees, Robert I.[212]	G	2nd Lt
Reeve, Horace M.[213]	I	Captain/ADC to Gen Bates
Rice, Edmund[214]	F&S	Major
Ross, Tenney[215]	G	1st Lt
Sample, William R.[216]	D/F&S	Commanding/Adjutant
Sharp, Bernard[217]	A/2nd Bn	Adjutant
Siviter, Francis P.[218]	Atch	Captain/41st Inf
Smith, Allen, Jr.[219]	I	1st Lt
Smith, Fred E.[220]	A	1st Lt

[211] Potter, of Ireland and Calif; Civil War veteran; enlisted under names Gerald Otway and Wm. H. Clayton, Private and Corporal I and K Companies, 13th New York Cavalry Oct 1863 to Feb 1865; private to 1st Sergt, 1st Cavalry, July 1866 to October 1869; Private, Third Inf, Sept 1870; Major and Surgeon of Volunteers June 1898; resigned Dec 1900; Major Surgeon of Vols Feb 1901; disch Nov 1902.

[212] Rees, of Michigan, Private and Corporal of Engineers 1897-1899; 2nd Lt Third Inf Oct 1899; 1st Lt 9 April 1901.

[213] Reeve, of Tennessee, USMA '92; Third Inf; 1st Lt April 1898; Capt Feb 1901; transfer to 17th Inf May 1902.

[214] Civil War veteran; As Major of the 19th Massachusetts Infantry, Rice helped repel Pickett's Charge at Gettysburg and was awarded the Medal of Honor. In July 1898, Rice was detached to serve in his brevet rank as Colonel of the 26th Infantry, U.S. Volunteers and later served as military governor of Panay. He returned to the U.S. in July 1901, retired in 1903 and died "very suddenly" of heart failure in August 1906 with the rank of brigadier general. He is buried in Arlington Cemetery.

[215] Ross, of NH and DC; 2nd Lt Third Inf July 1898; 1st Lt March 1899.

[216] Sample, of Tennessee and Arkansas, USMA '88; 14th Inf June 1888; Captain, Third Inf April 1899.

[217] Sharp, of Tennessee, Private thru Sergeant, Third Arty June 1895 to May 1899; 2nd Lt Third Inf April 1899; 1st Lt 27th Inf Feb 1901; transf back to Third Inf July 1901.

[218] Siviter, of Pennsylvania, USMA '95 12th Inf; 11th Inf May 1899; Capt 41st USV Inf Aug 1899; Capt (Regulars) 28th Inf Feb 1901.

[219] Smith, Jr. of South Dakota; Corporal 1st Washington Vol Inf, April 1898; 2nd Lt 9th Inf April 1899; 1st Lt Third Inf, Feb 1901.

[220] Smith, of Illinois and North Dakota, QM Sgt and Sgt Maj 1st ND Inf 1899; 1st Lt 36 USV Inf July 1899; 1st Lt Third Inf Feb 1901.

Smith, Hamilton A.[221]	G/F&S	Commanding Company /Commissary
Stetson, Frederic T.[222]	K	1st Lt
Stewart, Walter E., Jr.[223]	E	2nd Lt
Stogsdall, Ralph R.[224]	A	1st Lt
Stone, William C.[225]	2nd Bn	QM and CS
Titus, Frank H.[226]	Atch	Surgeon/Major
Todd, Charles C.[227]	D	2nd Lt
Walker, Philip E.M.[228]	C	1st Lt
Ware, Orville J.	F&S	Chaplain
Watson, Frank B.[229]	H	Captain
Williams, Arthur[230]	B/1st Bn	Captain/Commanding Bn
Wygant, Henry S.[231]	B	1st Lt/Commanding Co
Yeatman, Richard T.[232]	H	Captain

---

[221] Smith, of Florida and Georgia, USMA '93, Third Inf; 1st Lt April 1898; Capt Feb 1901.
[222] Stetson of Minnesota and NY, USMA '92; 1st Lt Third Inf April 1898; retired May 1900.
[223] Stewart, of New Jersey, 2nd Lt Third Inf April 1899; Resigned Jan 1901; died 4 March 1901.
[224] Stogsdall, of Indiana, USMA '94; 1st Lt to Third Inf Dec 1899; Captain 30th Inf Feb 1901.
[225] Stone, of Maryland, Private and Corporal, 2nd Cavalry August 1898; 2nd Lt Third Inf August 1900.
[226] Titus, of Ohio and California, Major and Surgeon of Volunteers January 1901; hon disch Dec 1902.
[227] Todd, of Texas, 2nd Lt Third Inf July 1898; 1st Lt 20th Inf March 1899; retired Dec 1901.
[228] Walker, of Virginia, 2nd Lt 16th Inf July 1898; 1st Lt Third Inf March 1899.
[229] Watson, of Virginia and New Jersey, USMA '95; 2nd Lt, 19th Inf; Captain, Third Inf March 1901.
[230] Williams, of Pennsylvania and Kentucky, 2nd Lt Third Inf Oct 1874; 1st Lt March 1885; Major 26th Inf Feb 1901; transf Third Inf Dec 1902.
[231] Wygant, of Texas, Private and Corporal, 6th Inf July 1897; 1st Lt 14th Inf March 1899; transf to Third Inf Oct 1899.
[232] Yeatman, of Ohio, USMA '72; 2nd Lt 14th Inf; Captain March 1892; trans to Third Inf Oct 1900; Major 22nd Inf Nov 1900.

Obituary for Major General James H. McRae
(from Arlington National Cemetery website)

JAMES MCRAE DIES; 'FIGHTING GENERAL '

Ex-Head of 2d Corps Area
Led the Lightning Division
In Meuse-Argonne Offensive

CLASSMATE OF
PERSHING

Indian Campaigner Decorated
for Gallantry
Under Fire in Cuba,
Philippines, France

BERKELEY, California, May 1, 1940 – Major General James H. McRae, U.S.A., Retired, died today at the age of 70. He served in the Indian Campaigns, the Spanish-American and World Wars and in the Philippine Insurrection.

General McRae commanded throughout the World War the Seventy-eighth Division, which took part in the St. Mihiel and the Meuse-Argonne Offensives.

Burial will be in the National Cemetery, Arlington, Virginia.
Known throughout the military service as "the fighting general," General McRae had one of the most distinguished military careers of any officer ever to serve in the United States Army. He served in nearly every part of the world where American troops have been stationed in the last half century, and received several decorations and other citations.

General McRae was particularly widely known in New York, where he commanded the Second Corps Area from November 21, 1920 to December 1, 1927, a few weeks before he retired. As commanding officer of the Seventy-eighth (Lightning) Division during the World War, his command included many troops from New York, although the bulk of them came from New Jersey, Delaware and several other States.

His leadership of the Seventy-eighth Division in the Meuse-Argonne Offensive in 1918 brought him the Distinguished Service Medal from the United States Government for "exceptionally meritorious and distinguished service." He also commanded this division during its training period in the United States and in France and in action in the battle of St. Mihiel, the Limney Sector and in other operations.

For gallantry in action in the battle of El Caney, Cuba, in the Spanish-American War, he received a Silver Star Citation, and a similar citation for gallantry in action at Mount Lumandan, Luzon, P. I. in the Philippine Insurrection.[233] Other World War decorations he held were the British Order of the Bath, the French Legion of Honor and the French Croix de Guerre with Palm.

He was born at Lumber City, Georgia on December 24, 1863 and was a classmate of General John J. Pershing at West Point, from which he graduated in 1886. For ten years after his graduation, he served in the Middle and Far West, helping to quell sporadic Indian uprisings.

Shortly after the United States declared war against Germany in 1917, he was made a Brigadier General and temporarily assigned to command the 158th Depot Brigade at Camp Sherman, Ohio. Later he was assigned to command the Ninth Infantry Brigade of the Fifth Division. On April 7, 1918, he was given command of the Seventy-eighty Division, then in training in Camp Dix, New Jersey, a command which he held for the remainder of the war.

General McRae commanded the United States Disciplinary Barracks at Fort Leavenworth, Kansas, in 1919 and in 1920 was Assistant Chief of Staff (G1) supervising Army Personnel at the War Department from September 1921...[H]e was given command of the Fifth Corps Area at Columbus, Ohio. From 1924 to 1926 he commanded the Philippine Department of the Army. He was in command of Ninth Corps Area with Headquarters at San Francisco for a time before coming to New York to command the Second Corps Area.

---

[233] **McRae's first Silver Star Citation was "for gallantry in action in the Santiago de Cuba Campaign, 22 June to 17 July 1898." The second citation "for gallantry in action during the Philippine Insurrection, 1899 to 1902"**

Brigadier General Edmund Rice

A Third Infantry Regiment officer, Rice was a Civil War Veteran, formerly of the 19th Massachusetts Infantry, who later saw service in the Philippines. In the Civil War he earned several brevets ending that conflict as a Lt Colonel.

He was awarded the Congressional Medal of Honor in 1891 for Civil War actions, specifically for leading his regiment in repelling Pickett's charge at the stone wall in Gettysburg. Wounded three times during the conflict, he was present at the Confederate surrender at Appomattox.

Rice was carried on the Third Infantry rolls as a Major but he didn't serve with them in the Philippines --- McKinley activated him to serve as a Colonel of U.S. Volunteers in the islands. In that capacity he led the 26th Infantry Regiment. He was named military governor of Panay (Visayas) in 1899 serving to 1901.

He retired from the Army on 14 August 1903 as Brigadier General. He is the inventor of the Rice Trowel and Rice Stacking Swivel. He died in 1906 and is buried in Section 3, Grave 1875 at Arlington Cemetery.

Roster of Enlisted Personnel

NCOs and Special Staff

Name	Unit	Rank
Armand, Charles	I	Cpl
Ayres, Leroy	Band	Sgt
Babman, August	Band	Cpl
Berg, Anton	F&S	Color Sgt
Blattner, William	I	Cpl
Breuer, John	H	Cpl
Brown, Guy E.	A	Sgt
Burns, Alexander T.	K	Sgt
Carson, George W.	M	Cpl
Chinclacoske, Edouard	Casual Det	Sgt
Chinsecki, Edmund	D	Cpl
Clark, Harry J.	G	Band
Clark, John J. A.	Regt	QM Sgt
Dahl, Ole A.	I	Cpl
Davidson, William	H	Cpl
Dehne, William L.	C	Sgt
Donea, Peter	A	Sgt
Drews, Charles	F	1st Sgt
Drimin, Daniel	Bn Staff	Sgt Major
Driver, Daniel H.	F&S	Sgt Major
Elder, Alvin E.	G	Cpl
Engdal, John	K	Cpl
Engdall, John	H	Sgt
Engelman, William	M	Sgt
Fagrie, Gary	M	Cpl
Fiedler, Crestof A.	F	Cpl
Fields, Frank	L	Sgt
Fields, Frank	F&S	Sgt Major
Frankoviki, Frank	M	Sgt
Geiser, Albert	F	Sgt
Gordon, John	L	Cpl
Grueindner, Anton	B	Cpl
Hanson, Morris C.	L	Cpl
Harry, Edward	Band	Chief Musician
Hart, Henry	F&S	Color Sgt
Hayden, Ernst	Bn Staff	Sgt Major
Helgren, Anton E.	F&S	Bn Sgt Major
Helker, John A.	F&S	Bn Sgt Major

Hollriegel, Jacob	K	1st Sgt
Hutcheson, Frank C.	I	Cpl
Hynes, Patrick S.	C	Sgt
Johnson, Albert S.	L	Cpl
Johnson, Albert S.	L	Cpl
Johnson, Edward	I	Sgt
Jones, Thomas	A	Sgt
Kaine, Patrick	D	1st Sgt
Kelly, Mark A.	L	Sgt
Kelly, Mark O.	L	Cpl
Kelly, Thomas	F&S	Commissary Sgt
Kelly, Thomas	F&S	Sgt
Kempton, George E.	Band	Cpl
Ketternan, August	A	Cpl
Kirtly, Nathan R.	L	Cpl
Knotowski, Peter	L	Cpl
Kochler, Henry	M	Sgt
Koehler, Henry	M	Sgt
Kristenike, Peter	L	Sgt
Larsen, Andrew C.	F&S	Bn Sgt Major
Leider, Albert	C	Sgt
Levine, Guss	C	Cpl
MacArthur, George	B	Sgt
Mackabee, William H.	I	Sgt
Markabee, William H.	I	Sgt
Martlick, Frank	A	1st Sgt
Matran, Hans	I	Cpl
Michalowski, Frank J.	C	Cook
Miller, Stephen	M	Sgt
Miller, Stephen/Steffen	M	Cpl
Monahan, John W.	Band	Drum Major
Monahan, John W.	Band	Sgt
Moon, Samuel P.	H	Sgt
Moore, William E.	C	1st Sgt
Morgan, Frank B.	I	Cpl
Morrison, George	Band	Cpl
Nation, John	Casual Det	Sgt
Nelson, Alexander	L	Cpl
Nelson, Alexander	Bn Staff	Sgt Major
Novatney, Joseph	L	Sgt
O'Conner, Maurice	I	Sgt
Peterson, Johannes	E	1st Sgt
Reeves, Edgar L.	I	Sgt

Reynolds, Elliot D.	A	Sgt
Riedd, Paul	I	Cpl
Safford, Frank	L	Cpl
Schneider, Albert J.	H	Sgt
Sorlemam, August	Cook	M
Start, John G.	E	Sgt
Taylor, James P.	L	Cpl
Teck, Benjamin F.	A	Cpl
Vanderputter, Charles L.	G	Musician
Washington, William T.	Band	Sgt
Whiteside, Dan W.	I	Cpl
Williams, Milton	L	Cpl
Williard, Andrew J.	A	Sgt
Wright, Charles L.H.	L	Cpl
Wyatt, Richard P.	K	Sgt
Young, John C.	F&S	Color Sgt
Young, John C.	L	Sgt
Young, John C.	Band	Sgt Major

Privates – By Last Name

Name[234]	Co
Aaron, Charles T.	F
Abbott, Lewis	L
Abbott, William	L
Abetz, Louis	M
Abramowitz, Sam	A
Adams, Allen P.	E
Adams, Bernard E.	D
Adams, James M.	L
Adams, Ollie W.	F
Adams, Samuel J.	I
Adams, Warren	M
Adams, William H.	G
Adler, Charles	C
Ainsworth, Joseph	C
Alber, Job E.	I
Albrecht, Thomas	F
Alexander, Frank	M
Alexander, Nathan T.	D
Alexander, Percey N.	D
Allen, Albert	A
Allen, Charles	M
Allen, Fred L.	D
Allen, George W.	B
Allen, Jerry R.	L
Allen, Oliver	B
Allenton, Lee G.	G
Allerton, Emas A.	F
Alley, Charles O.	E
Alpert Joe	F
Aluncher, George A.	E
Amman, Charles	I
Amster, Max W.	M
Anderson, Fred	C
Anderson, Fred P.	H
Anderson, George W.	F
Anderson, Harlie	E
Anderson, John S.	A
Anderson, Peter M.	A
Anderson, Stanley	C
Ansborn, Nathan	D
Arin, Edward	L
Armitage, Elliot B.	C
Armstrong, Willis	H
Arniss, James E.	M
Arnold, Harry J.	I
Atkinson, Othello Q.	D
Austin, Edward C.	C
Avery, John	G
Ayres, Leory	C
Babler, John	D
Backer, James	B
Badford	E?
Bailey, Frank	K
Bailey, George	L
Bailey, William J.	E
Baird, Orival W.	H
Baker, Allen	K
Baker, Fred A.	F
Baker, George H.	E
Baker, Jacob E.	K
Baker, James H.	K
Baker, John	C
Balback, John H.	H
Baldwin, John	D
Balke, Edward	I
Ballach, William S.	G
Balliand, George A.	H
Balsh, Thomas B.	I
Banado, Amable W.	F
Barger, Harry P.	A
Barker, Joseph	C
Barmand, Warren E.	L
Barnes, John	M
Barrett, James S.	K
Barrett, Thomas	H
Bartlett, George	L

---

[234] Some of the names were difficult to determine due to handwriting styles making transcribing difficult.

Bates, Guy F.	L	Blickel, John	M
Bates, Harry E.	M	Bliss, Harry K.	A
Bates, James H.	E	Blodgett, George W.	E
Battis, John	A	Bloom, Henry C.	D
Baugh, Rufus B.	L	Bobb, Henry	F
Bauman, Edward	E	Bobo, Benjamin E	A
Baxter, Frank	B	Bochulein, Max	A
Baxter, Harry M.	B	Bockson, Anton	G
Bay, Fred	D	Boeslew, Ludlow	F
Beaman, Philip	B	Boggess, Robert E. L.	G
Beau, Bert P.	D	Bolender, George B.	B
Becher, Henry	G	Boltinghause,	
Beck, George E.	F	Christopher	B
Beeson, William	G	Bond, James	E
Begley, John	K	Booker, Emil	A
Beier, Charles H.	K	Boon, Francis M.	M
Beisinger, A.L.	E	Booth, Harry	M
Beison, Herbert E.	H	Booth, John H.	G
Belanger, Alfred	H	Boring, William A.	F
Belanger, Napoleon	H	Borland, George R.	M
Bemen, Cecile T.	A	Bornfield, Julius	B
Benjamin, Percie E.	M	Borson, Arthur	M
Bennett, George	H	Bowles, Jesse R.	C
Bennett, William A.	A	Bowling, Charles D.	C
Benson, Alex	L	Bowls, Jessie R.	C
Benson, George B.	G	Bowring, John F.	D
Benson, John	K	Bowring, John F.	D
Berchirt, Charles A.	L	Boyce, Walter	K
Berg, Anton	D	Boyd, Alberson W.	M
Bergdall, Charles	B	Boyd, Hugh H.	M
Betterton, Philip	A	Boyd, Samuel J.	M
Beuman, Edward	E	Boyden, John A.	A
Bevan, James M.	M	Boyle, John D.	E
Bevan, Oscar	F	Boyle, John D.	G
Bierman, Owen	H	Boyle, John D.	G
Bittenbender, Aaron	M	Bradshaw, Masten	A
Black, Bernard D.	M	Brady, James F.	I
Black, Charles D.	E	Brasher, Fred I.	A
Black, William	M	Bray, John S.	E
Blackwell, Joseph B.	B	Brazil, Michael	A
Blair, William	F	Breed, Charles H.	C
Blanton, Benton T.	I	Breeding, Samuel B.	G
Blasdel, Ira	G	Brefker, Anthony	A

Breman, James	A		Buckner, Edward A.	K
Bremer, John	H		Budd, William H.	K
Brenthinger, Claude M.	M		Buins, Alexander	H
Breur, George G.	G		Bundly, Reginald W.	A
Brewer, Albert	E		Bunting, William	G
Breyer, Henry F.	E		Burke, David	A
Briehry, Henry	H		Burke, George H.	E
Brier, Mahew	I		Burn, John O.	G
Bright, David H.	K		Burnett, Ross A.	I
Brilie, Samuel R.	E		Burns, Edward F.	I
Bringhaus, Homer A.	M		Burns, Frank	L
Brockman, John F.	C		Burns, Michael J.	G
Brohen, Emant	I		Burst, Herman	H
Bronson, William J.	A		Burton, Robert H.	E
Brooke, Marion W.	C		Busch, John	G
Brooks, Charles	F		Butler, Irwin H.	K
Brooks, Charles	I		Butmeister, Henry	I
Brooks, Mark E.	C		Butts, Benjamin P.	B
Brorontey, Elmer	M		Butz, Frank B.	G
Bross, William	K		Buzzard, John W.	I
Brown, Arthur R.	L		Byrd, Frederick	G
Brown, Bancroft	D		Byrd, James W.	C
Brown, Clint	G		Cachart, Edwin C.	L
Brown, Edward H.	A		Cadle, Jeff	G
Brown, Fred S.	D		Cadotte, George	C
Brown, George G.	E		Calkins, Charles	E
Brown, James M.	F		Callahan, Thomas	C
Brown, John	A		Callahan, William J.	H
Brown, John	I		Cameron, Alexander A.	A
Brown, Thomas A.	K		Cameron, James A.	E
Brown, W. Scott	E		Cameron, James R.	E
Browning, Frank	D		Cameron, John F.	L
Bruce, Eugene W.	L		Campbell, Henry P.	E
Bruger, Henry	L		Campbell, John	B
Brumag, George	K		Campbell, John	I
Brundy, Fred	G		Campbell, Percy F.	M
Bryan, Guy C.	H		Campbell, Thomas	L
Bryant, Georgs	H		Candill, S.L.	F
Bryarly, Joseph L	E		Cannon, Joseph A.	A
Buchanan, James	H		Carey, John J.	C
Buchen, Frank	M		Carlson, Fritz C.	E
Buckley, Horatius	B		Carman, Charles S.	B
Buckley, Patrick M.	H		Carnery, Michael	C

Carney, John S.	K	Clemons, Alex H.	C
Carpenter, John H.	I	Cleveland, Eugen I.	B
Carr, Frank	I	Clifford, John	H
Carroll, Charles H.	G	Clinton, Charles A.	K
Carroll, Daniel J.	C	Clontina, Ernest	C
Carroll, Richard	B	Cloon, David F.	C
Carroll, William	I	Clothier, Clarence R.	L
Carroll, William F.	H	Clothier, Robert K.	L
Carter, Dawson	E	Coblusar, Christ.	E
Carter, Robert N.	F	Cogan, John H.	F
Carver, Henry	C	Cole, William	H
Cassidy, John A.	I	Coleman, Charles W.	D
Cassidy, Michael	C	Coleman, William	E
Catchings, William A.	G	Collan, James D.	H
Cauble, Thomas O.	D	Collins, James H.	A
Ceoon, Carl	H	Collins, John	K
Cerx, John B.	E	Collins, Max B.	K
Chambliss, Samuel M.	K	Collins, William H.	G
Champlis, Walter G.	D	Comer, Arthur J.	M
Chapman, Frank P.	F	Comerly, John F.	K
Chapman, Wesley R.	G	Compton, John L.	C
Charles, Clarence S.	M	Coney, Edward B.	C
Cheatham, William	H	Conley, Perry A.	F
Chiller, James I.	M	Connaughton, John F.	C
Chrice, James	D	Conner, George	E
Christoph, Joseph	K	Conner, John F.	B
Church, Guy I.	K	Conners, Dan	D
Cindiff, Benjamin F.	M	Conners, Thomas J.	M
Clannich, Daniel	B	Conroy, James	B
Clarenback, Fredrick W.	K	Considine, Richard	M
Clark, Charles A.	F	Converse, Frank	C
Clark, Edwin S.	H	Convery, Patrick J.	K
Clark, Frank, Jr.	H	Conway, Martin	C
Clark, Joel	C	Cook, Clare. R.	G
Clark, John	B	Cook, Frank H.	D
Clark, John A.	K	Cook, Glen O.	H
Clark, Peter	E	Cooley, James J.	
Clark, William G.		Cooley, James J.	D
Clark, William G.	J	Cooper, Lindley M	D
Clark, William M.	L	Copley, James A.	F
Clarke, Thomas	L	Coppard, Sydney	M
Clayton, Charles D.	M	Courtney, James	E
Claywell, Joseph	L	Courtright, Harry W.	B

Cox, John B.		Decker, Bertram S.	D
Crabtree, Ulysses H.	M	DeHart, Charles C.	M
Crain, Virgil E.	B	DeHart, Christopher	L
Craine, Charles	I	Demanway, William	C
Craw, Herman E.	H	Dement, Jesse J.	E
Crawford, Hugh	L	Demick, Orlie	G
Crawford, William	C	Dempsey, John J.	C
Crego, Oscar	L	Denizin, Arthur	K
Croft, Claude	G	Dennis, David C.	F
Crour, Eugene	J	Denton, David W.	M
Crowe, Edward M.	I	Derwin, William H.	C
Crowe, John A.	C	Devires, James H.	A
Crump, Walter W.	K	Devlin, George	M
Cuill, William	B	Dewar, John	G
Culbertson, Frank E.	H	Dickinson, Theodore	E
Cullatson, Augustus B.	K	Diess, Emil	K
Culley, James B.	C	Dietrich, Crl	H
Cummings, Frank	D	Dilgard, Quinby A.	G
Cummings, Peter	F	Dilger, Leonhard L.	L
Cummings, William B.	A	Diller, Williams S.	D
Daley, John F.	C	Dillman, August	L
Dalton, Marten	C	Dillon, James E.	H
Daniby, Michael	E	Dillon, William	B
Daniels, Edwin G.	F	Dink, Fred	G
Dannall, Daniel	L	Dobrosky, Joseph	D
Darns, Thomas	E	Dobson, Frank	F
Dauding, Roy	H	Doherty, Michael J.	H
Daughess, Jess H.	A	Dole, Martin	C
Dauphin, Walter A.	H	Doltoh, William	K
Davan, Patrick	L	Donaldson, Joseph	B
Davenport, Richard	L	Donlon, John	D
Davidson, James W.	H	Donnlevy, James	E
Davis, Clarence A.	A	Dorge, Henry	H
Davis, Garth W.	F	Douglas, Earl W.	E
Davis, Henry D.	B	Doyle, William	L
Davis, Hugh L.	L	Draper, Charles R.	G
Davis, Joseph H.	M	Dries, Theodore	K
Davis, Lewis	K	Driver, Edward C.	L
Davis, Samuel J.	B	Drum, Hugh R.	
Dawley, Raph M.	K	Drury, William	M
Dea, Charles	C	Duffy, Joseph	C
Deamer, George	K	Duffy, Michael	C
Debats, Met. M.	M	Dugan, John L.	E

Name	Co.	Name	Co.
Dullaghan, Clarence D.	E	Estes, Charles E.	F
Dullaghan, Frank R.L.	E	Evans, Charles	M
Dulsigg, James	F	Evans, John K.	H
Dunbar, John G.	G	Evans, Philip	E
Dunbar, Roy S.	G	Everett, James A.	F
Duncan, Charles E.	B	Fagersrom, Charles	E
Dunham, George E.	I	Falkner, James L.	F
Dunlap, Harry G.	G	Farmer, John M.	L
Dunn, John L.		Farnum, Samuel W.	A
Dunn, Michael	B	Farrell, William O.	
Dunn, William	H	Farrell, William P.	A
Dunnaway, William	C	Fasbender, Christopher	I
Dupont, George E.	C	Fawcell, James	D
Dyer, Charlie	D	Fawcett, Howard M.	L
Dyson, Benjamin W.	L	Fedalen, Paul	G
Eaglon, William	G	Fehan, John	K
Earne, Walter T.	E	Feldon, George	B
Earnshaw, Albert H.	B	Fellman, Frank	L
Easterday, Lawrence	E	Fellows, George	F
Eberling, Frank	C	Fenike, Ernst	F
Ebert, Otto	G	Fenn, Thomas S.	C
Eckhert, Romairs	A	Fenster, Mooheim	H
Eddy, William	G	Fenton, Charles M.	M
Edgeworth, James G.	F	Ferguson, Clarence H.	H
Edmonds, William	D	Ferguson, Smith	F
Edwards, William	D	Ferguson, Walter E.	F
Egan, Joseph	E	Ferrill, Willima F.	E
Eggenberger, William	K	Fields, Ira	F
Ehringast, Albret J.	E	Filiatreault, Paul E.	E
Eiler, William L.	C	Fillbrand, Fred G.	E
Eillis, William H.	L	Fillman, George	A
Elam, Henry L.	F	Fink, Lester L.	H
Eldridge, Clement	B	Finn, John E.	F
Ellis, William H.	L	Finnegan, Henry M.	A
Embler, Walter H.	D	Fischer, Sonis	F
Enderline, Theodore	A	Fisher, Clyde C.	L
Engdal, John	H	Fisher, Frank J.	B
Engel, Frederick G.	B	Fisher, Jacob	G
English, George R.	A	Fitzel, John A.	B
Ensidel, Albert H.	H	Fitzgerald, Andrew G.	K
Erwin, William B.	E	Fitzgerald, William E.	M
Estabrook, Elmer O.	L	Fitzgerald, William H.	M
Esterly, Jacob R.	J	Fitzpatrick, John	K

Flanagan, Thomas	F		Gaddey, Charles	H
Flemming, Elmer O.	M		Gaddy, Chanler	H
Flemming, Frank	C		Gallagher, James P.	F
Fletcher, Ralph H.	E		Galland, Alexis	A
Fletcher, William J.	K		Galligan, Henry P.	A
Folk, Henry E.	I		Gamble, Charles G.	C
Fonder, William E.	M		Gammon, George H.	I
Foole, Michael	E		Gannon, James G.	F
Forbes, Burton F.	D		Gardner, Frank W.	L
Forbes, Harry	C		Gardner, John D.	D
Ford, Frank H.	A		Gardner, Noah E.	G
Ford, Patrick J.	F		Gatens, Peter	D
Ford, Robert H.	B		Gates, Bert E.	I
Ford, Wallace H.	H		Gauman, Emil	E
Fordyce, Bliss P.	C		Gelb, John	D
Fordyce, Charles	G		Georing, Reimer	E
Forrester, Richard S.	F		Gibbs, John H.	F
Foster, William	A		Gibbs, Ulysses F.	E
Fourney, Hermann C.	E		Gibson, John	F
Fowler, Mat J.	A		Gibson, Pearl	M
Fox, Michael	M		Gilberdt, Ona B.	E
Frank, Richard T.	C		Gilgen, Albert	K
Frankowski, Frank	M		Ginto, Bent I.	L
Frantchi, Adolph	M		Glass, William F.	F
Frantz, George F.	K		Glazier, Leo J.	B
Frase, John G.	A		Glencoe, Harry W.	B
Fraska, Paul	L		Glendon, Harry P.	K
Fraze, Donald K.	A		Glenn, Patrick	F
Frazen, Jay B.	A		Goll, John T.	C
Frear, Warren D.	I		Gordon, Archie H.	K
Free, Frederick E.	G		Gordon, James G.	L
Freeman, Samuel P.	F		Gordon, Victor D.	F
French, Frank D.	M		Gorman, John A.	A
Frey, Joseph	G		Gosling, Isaac	H
Frisbie, Floyd I.	A		Graden, Charles J.	K
Frost, Andrew W.	F		Graff, George	L
Fryer, James B.	I		Graff, William V.	F
Fryman, Otto N.	F		Gragert, John	K
Fullwiler, Lewis	K		Graham, Charles C.	G
Fuss, Frederick	G		Graham, George J.	B
Fuss, Frederick W.	D		Graham, John	M
Gabeatzki, August	D		Grahech, George A.	H
Gabsour, Mitre	F		Grammon, John E.	A

Grant, Peter S.	M		Hamlin, George S.	M
Gray, Charles	H		Hamm, Andrew	C
Gray, Harry C.	G		Hammer, Charles	L
Gray, James	H		Hanike, Steven	B
Green, Bert	D		Hansen, Criss	C
Green, Lonis	F		Hansen, Peter C.	K
Greenberg, Bernard	F		Hansen, Vall D.	F
Greenhill, David M.	F		Hanson, Christ E.	K
Greenhood, Bernard A.	F		Haragin, John	K
Gregory, James	G		Harbig, Joseph	B
Greives, Lundy Lee	C		Harding, William P.	G
Griffin, William	B		Hardy, Albert Hardy	K
Griger, Lewis	C		Hark, Henry	K
Grigiss, William H.	G		Harkins, Daniel O.	L
Grim, Albert	A		Harkins, John	D
Grimes, Albert F.	E		Harlow, Honier S.	H
Grimm, William J.	D		Harmand, Mont	E
Grissom, Paul H.	G		Harmoan, David	A
Grogham, Vincent	D		Harmons, David H.	D
Gross, Sidney	G		Harper, Edward J.	C
Grubbs, Edgar S.	B		Harre, Harry P.	E
Grumble, Frederick A.	H		Harrigan, James M.	E
Grummings, John	F		Harris, Charles	H
Grunewald, Emil F.	C		Harris, Everett B.	D
Guerriceo, Andrew	K		Harris, James W.	H
Guilmette, Alexis	G		Harris, John C.	F
Gullagher, Hugh J.	G		Harrison, Clayton A.	A
Gullett, Frank B.	I		Harrison, George	C
Gust, H.S.	B		Harrison, Peter C.	E
Gustaves, Harry	H		Harrison, Victor	H
Haas, George W.	H		Harrison, William C.	K
Haase, Otto	M		Harrison, William E.	K
Hager, Robert	C		Harry, William H.	H
Haggart, John F.	K		Harney, John F.	L
Haines, Thomas A.	F		Harvey, Roy	H
Hainke, Rudolph	L		Harvey, Waldo E.	H
Halback, Jacob H.	F		Haskell, Frank H.	L
Halberg, Gustav L.	I		Haslein, William R.	L
Hall, Jesse N.	D		Hassant, Horatio H.	G
Hallbe, Edward L.	A		Hassey, William H.	E
Halligan, Henry P.			Hattabaugh, Frank E.	H
Hamilton, Burton H.	E		Hatten, Clarence E.	D
Hamilton, Jack	E		Haug, Aksel H.	M

Hauley, Vincent	B	Hiliard, Joseph H.	A
Hauser, , Hans B.	I	Hillinger, Robert A.	C
Hausworth, Benjamin F.	C	Himmelbach, William	K
Hawes, William E.	E	Hines, John T.	K
Hawkins, Samuel W.	F	Hippler, Charles L.	G
Haworth, Benjamin F.	C	Hishman, Aug. J.	A
Hayes, Claude S.	D	Hix, John F.	D
Hayes, George W.	F	Hobbs, Leroy	I
Hayes, John W.	C	Hobren, Peter	E
Hayes, William E.	H	Hochley, Edward W.	L
Hayes, William W.	I	Hocking, William J.	H
Haynes, Irving G.	E	Hockley, Edward N.	L
Hayse, Lewis H.	C	Hodges, John W.	B
Healy, Martin	E	Hoffman, Arther F.	B
Heberling, William H.	G	Hoge, Ole D.	H
Heffernan, Joseph F.	A	Hohe, John D.	H
Heisen, Arthur	G	Hohnberg, B.C.E.	H
Hellen, William A.	A	Holacken, Fred	A
Helm, William C.	D	Holgreen, Augie	A
Helms, Clarence E.	G	Hollen, Elmer C.	K
Helser, Palmer	H	Hollman, Horace	H
Helton, Charles	H	Holmes, Henry C.	H
Helun, Palmer	H	Holssiche, M.C.	G
Hempstead, Arthur	F	Holzer, Fred W.	C
Henderson, Daniel A.	F	Homer, Charles B.	F
Hendrichs, John	H	Hoost, George	E
Hennesey, Daniel J.	D	Hopkins, William R.	F
Henning, Frank	M	Hoppensett, Isaac B.	E
Henry, Merrick B.	H	Horst, George	C
Hensley, Hack	E	Horton, Edwin C.	L
Herbert, Otto J.	C	Horton, John D.	M
Herman, John J.	C	Horton, Walter C.	L
Herrick, William A.	E	Hoskins, John B.	I
Hester, James	H	Houndshill, Finley	I
Heston, Ernest C.	B	Hovey, LeRoy	H
Hickey, Edward	D	Howard, John F.	E
Hicks, Harry	E	Howr, Walter H.	B
Hicks, Jess F.	D	Hubbard, Millard	I
Hicks, William J.	C	Huber, Peter J.	H
Higgins, Daniel	G	Hudleston, William	A
Higgins, Peter	H	Huebner, Fred F.	E
Hight, James W.	G	Huff, Marion S.	C
Hightower, Avery F.	G	Hugill, Lewis	L

Huk, Pretz	H		Johnson, Lloyd M	D
Hulbright, Jacob	K		Johnson, Martin	D
Hull, Frederick R.	G		Johnson, Robert S.	H
Hull, Ira E.	B		Johnson, William R.	L
Hummer, Daniel J.	D		Jones, Archibald H.	E
Hunt, Arthur L.	K		Jones, Cateb/Caleb	M
Huntley, Carl	H		Jones, Frank O.	D
Huntzinger, Paul	I		Jones, Henry E.	E
Hurley, James	H		Jones, John O.	M
Hurst, Arther S.	K		Jones, Ulysess G.	D
Hurston, George B.	L		Jones, Wiley	L
Hurt, Stephen T.	K		Jones, William T.	E
Hurt, William A.	D		Jordan, John	K
Huston, Frank H.	L		Josten, Christ.	B
Hutchins, Lewis J.	L		Joyce, Edward	H
Hutton, Washington	D		Joyce, Mathew J.	H
Ingham, Thomas L.	G		Jullianan, James M	G
Irving, George C.	H		Just, Louis C.	B
Iwantz, Frederick A.	H		Kachler, Sonis G.	H
Jackel, Walter D.	G		Kane, John	M
Jackson, Albert B.	B		Kane, John J.	E
Jackson, Jefferson T.	I		Kappham, Gustave	D
Jackson, Karl E.	B		Karger, Charles	M
Jackson, Lee	A		Karsch, Henry G.	A
Jackson, Max	C		Karzinski, Anton	M
Jacobs, John E.	G		Kaska, Julius	I
Jakaluski, Frank	M		Kazmer, George	G
Janoska, Joseph	E		Kearney, James	M
January, James H.	L		Keating, John H.	A
Jarke, William	I		Kehoe, James	B
Jeffers, Walter R.	B		Keller, Hans A.	I
Jensen, Conrad	M		Keller, William J.	F
Jenson, Walter	I		Kelly, David F.	H
Jepson, William F.C.	A		Kelly, Edwin	E
Jerres, Wichert C.	F		Kelly, James B.	H
Jindrich, Joseph	H		Kelly, John J.	I
Johnson, Albert S.	M		Kelly, Patrick	M
Johnson, Charles	H		Kelly, William J.	F
Johnson, George	B		Kelsh, William D.	C
Johnson, James	G		Kennen, William C.	I
Johnson, John E.	M		Kennerly, Arthur F.	B
Johnson, John O.	H		Kenney, John E.	I
Johnson, Lewis T.	B		Kent, William S.	K

Kerns, William M.	D	Lafferty, Barney	G
Kerries, Daniel F.	E	Lafond, Felix J.	G
Kershaw, John J	B	Laird, john M.	A
Kesy, Donald	F	Lambert, Frederick J.	A
Kindell, Louis W.	C	Lambert, James F.	
King, Mike A.	A	Lamon, Isaac J.	G
Kinigl, Joseph	I	Lamont, Charles	I
Kirby, William	I	Landers, Curtis	C
Kirnan, Pierce P.	F	Landes, Phillip	D
Kirwan		Lane, Clarence	L
Kistler, Robert C.	B	Lane, Webster	K
Kittel, Louis	M	Langford, Charles S.	J
Klein, George	L	Lanier, Frank	A
Klemer, Edward W.	F	Larchet, Danine	I
Klepsher, John A.E.	I	Larkin, Edward P.	L
Klinkhammer, Anthony F.	I	Larkin, Timothy J.	I
		Larson, Andrew C.	C
Knapp, Russell S.	B	Larson, Louis	M
Know, Alexander	D	Larson, Oscar M.	M
Koehler, Chalres	I	Larson, Peter	K
Kohanek, Peter	I	Larson, William	A
Kohank, John	M	Lasenbly, Guy	G
Kohl, William J.	E	Lauderman, Meyr	C
Konicka, Steven		Laurence, Guy C.	I
Kont, William S.	K	Lawton, John J.	A
Kooheler, Louis	D	Leach, Arthur J.	M
Koppe, Richard F.	I	Leach, Fred W.	K
Kortinatis, William	I	Leaman, James C.	F
Koschnitzki, August H.	H	Leanard, Milton	H
Kostenbaden, John N.	K	Leasch, Arthur J.	M
Kramer, Joseph	L	Lease, Fred A.	B
Krehser, August	L	Leash, William H.	D
Krohn, William	B	Leber, Edward W.	F
Krolskowski, Leonidas	B	Lee, John T.	A
Krouse, Frank	G	Leeding, Irvin	G
Krueger, Fred	K	Legate, Clyde	L
Krueger, Otto	L	Legerwood, Benjamin	H
Kuhlsubach, Louis H.	A	Lehman, Henry	M
Kunchel, Nicholas	F	Leidy, John F.	D
Kuney, Walter G.	M	Leisboken, Melvin P.	L
LaBeau, Joseph F.	E	Lellwig, Andrew	L
Lacey, Thomas H.	I	LeMay, William	F
Lafayette, William A.	A	Lemery, Maurice	K

Lenn, Harry W.	K		Marksen, Otto	G	
Levy, Benjamin F.	I		Marrow, Vincenzo T.	I	
Lewis, Schuyler, C.	B		Marshall, Fred D.	E	
Lichtainwalter, Frank B.	M		Martenson, Hagbart	H	
Lillian, William J	D		Martin, Charles R.	F	
Lindeman, Henry J.	M		Martin, Frank	M	
Linden, Samuel C.	B		Martin, Frank C.	L	
Lindequist, John	M		Martin, Lewis		
Link, Julius J.	C		Martin, Lewis	D	
Linn, William	B		Martin, Thad J.	M	
Linn, William	D		Mason, Alfred S.	I	
Linney, Benjamin	I		Mattox, Louis W.	G	
Linning, Clarence J.	K		Mauz, Peter	F	
Lirenby, Crowl T.	G		May, Frank J.	E	
Lloyd P. Richard	G		Mayer, August J.	L	
Lockman, Herman	E		Mayhen, Alfred W.	L	
Logan, John H.	F		Maynard, Andrew R.	L	
Lomis, Jesse E.	A		Maynard, Leslie P.	L	
Loveless, Cortes	L		Mays, Charles E.	F	
Luke, Benjamin	D		McAndrews, Thomas	H	
Lundrum, Benton W.	I		McCain, John	D	
Lusk, Joseph E.	L		McCaine, Patric	B	
Lymes, James G.	G		McCandless, Lucien	L	
Lynch, Thomas	G		McCarthy, Felix	L	
Madden, David	F		McCarthy, Richard B.	M	
Madden, Harry	B		McCartney, George A.	A	
Maddocks, Edgar H.	I		McCartney, George A.	F	
Mahoney, Michael J.	B		McCarty, Elijah A.	E	
Maier, Julius O.	K		McCarty, George A.	G	
Mainz, James E.	H		McChasney, Charles	G	
Makin, F.J.	A		McClean, Robert P.	H	
Malancon, Fred S.	M		McClure, John L.	M	
Maley, Joseph R.	E		McCormack, Arthur H.	K	
Malley, Simon O.	G		McCormick, Edward D.	M	
Mallory, John J.	I		McCory, Willam	K	
Malony, John P.	K		McCracken, John	D	
Maloy, Frank	D		McCracken, Joseph C.	H	
Mamet, George	L		McCrea, Donald C.	F	
Mangam, Joseph T.E.	G		McCullluogh, Millard C.	M	
Manz, Peter	F		McDaniel, Louis C.	G	
March, Claude A.	M		McDonald, Perry	H	
Marchank, Joseph J.	I		McDonald, Walter	K	
Marin, Philias	K		McDonald, William A.	C	

McDonough, Bernard	F	Miller, Clifford A.	F
McDouls, Alexander J.	D	Miller, David	L
McFarlan, Edward	K	Miller, Frank F.	C
McGinnes, Joseph M.	M	Miller, Frederick	F
McGover, Charles	E	Miller, Frederick	L
McGovern, James	L	Miller, Lucas A.	F
McGroary, Michael	K	Miller, William	A
McGuinny, Michael M.	L	Miller, William	C
McGuire, Edward	K	Millerick, George F.	I
McGuire, Rodney S.	K	Millman, Harry C.	K
McGuire, Ser W.	I	Milton, William	D
McGuire, Thomas J.	D	Mitchell, Alexander	H
McGuire, Walter J.	B	Mitchell, Charles	C
McHugh, Lawrence C.	M	Moehrle, Philip	G
McKaunnin, Ambrose T.	F	Molarkey, Dennis	H
McKnight, James	F	Mometz, William O.	L
McKnight, James		Monaghs, Thomas	A
McLaughlin, John	A	Monahan, Leslie	H
McLaughlin, John	H	Monghan, William J	I
McLaughlin, Patrick J.	K	Monroe, Frederick,	L
Mclure, William S.	K	Mooney, George	K
Mcmahon, John J.	K	Moore, John D	F
McNave, Robert	B	Moore, Perry	G
McNight, Joseph P.	M	Moore, Samuel P.	H
McPhee, John	F	Moorecheau, Thomas	H
Mears, Frederick	K	Moose, Thomas B.	
Meehan, Hugh F.	H	Morgan, Hugh	K
Melby, William	L	Morgan, John W.	I
Mennon, John	C	Morris, Albert V.	A
Mercer, William F.	M	Morris, Robert S.	K
Merrill, Williard J.	M	Morrison, Edward R.	K
Merritt, Harry O.	E	Morrissey, Michael	K
Metz, Harry E.	K	Mosher, Edward	A
Metzger, William R.	B	Motchman, Frederick	K
Meyer, Charles W.	D	Motter, John H.	A
Meyers, Charles H.	K	Mounty, William B.	L
Meyers, Fred	D	Mullen, Patrick	G
Meyers, Frederick E.	K	Muller, John	I
Meyers, Henry	L	Muller, Patrick	G
Meyers, Oliver O.	G	Mullin, Martin J.	J
Midorelle, Martin E.	I	Mullins, Thomas	I
Midville, Mike E.	I	Munson, Marten	I
Milan, Charles H.	L	Murphy, Frank	G

Murphy, James L.	M	Obenshain, Guy W.	M
Murphy, Patrick J.	A	O'Brien, David J.	F
Murphy, Peter J.	K	O'Brien, Evertt	E
Murphy, Thomas	D	O'Brien, William	C
Murray, Eddie	H	O'Coner, Lawrence	G
Murray, Michael T.	G	O'Donnell, John	L
Murray, Ronnie	E	Oedekoven, Frank	L
Murray, Thomas	K	Oelkers, Dietrich	A
Music, Stephen	K	O'Grady, James F.	L
Mutek, William	B	O'Hanlon, James F.	L
Myers, Charles C.	F	O'Hara, Merlin F.	D
Myers, Phillip	C	Olsen, Emil J.	G
Nadle, Charles B.	I	Olson, Hans L.	K
Nagle, Michael	H	Olson, Ole	H
Nation, John	B	O'Malley, Michael	E
Natshak, Joseph	L	O'Neil, Frank	K
Neatm Henry J.	G	O'Neil, Thomas L.	K
Needham, Edward H.	K	O'Neil, William	H
Neely, Hermann	E	Orner, Wilson A.	D
Nelson, John H.	K	Orr, Eugene K.	L
Nelson, Joseph	C	Osborn, Charles A.	L
Nelson, Louis W.	H	Osborn, John J.	L
Nelson, Nels	G	Osinski, Casimir	I
Neumuller, Fred	H	Ott, George	F
Nevetry, Joseph	L	Owens, George S.	F
Newbert, Williams	D	Pabst, Frederick	L
Newman, Frank	F	Packer, George	C
Newman, John	L	Page, George	A
Nickell, Noah C.	G	Paige, Robert	D
Nickerson, Henry A.	E	Palmer, Frank A.	L
Nieman, George	E	Parcell, David J.	K
Nieman, George	E	Pardee, Fred C.	D
Nisbet, George	B	Parker, Charles E.	K
Noble, Charles W.	C	Parker, Frank	G
Nordstrom, Charles	B	Parker, Henry W.	
Nordstrom, Louis	G	Parker, James R.	I
Norman, John J.	G	Parker, Patrick J.	G
Norman, Sanford, W.	D	Parkinson, William	K
Norris, Thomas P.	M	Parrott, John W.	M
Noss, Henry	D	Patterson, David K.	H
Novak, Frank A.	M	Patterson, Emery H.	C
Numandin, Henry	L	Patterson, Joseph C.	L
Oatman, John O.	G	Patton, Frank A.	K

Patton, Milburn	L			Posey, Jessie J.	C	
Patzke, Frederick	e			Pounder, Henry	H	
Payne, Charles	K			Powers, Walter S.	M	
Peachouse, Squire	L			Prader, John L.	M	
Peak, Ashley	F			Pratt, Frank V.	M	
Pearce, Robert A.	D			Precise, Jonathan	C	
Pearcy, Abraham	M			Premier, Dominic	L	
Pearson, James	A			Prescott, Ernest H.	E	
Peck, George	A			Priston, Harry A.	L	
Pendergast, William J.	B			Privett, Sylvan	K	
Pennington, James	I			Provenance, Charles C.	D	
Pensniger, John S.	H			Prubrick, H.	F	
Perkins, Allen	E			Pugh, George D.	C	
Perring, William E.	G			Pulver, Harry	B	
Persico, Dominic	L			Pundzia, George	D	
Perslach, Hugh	B			Quigley, John G.	B	
Person, Loyle	E			Quirck, Richard	E	
Peters, Charles A.	F			Rabb, Herbert	L	
Peters, James H.	F			Radford, Lewis	E	
Peterson, Charles A.	K			Radke, August	D	
Peterson, George	C			Ragan, William P.	I	
Peterson, Gustav	H			Rahfeld, Fred	C	
Peterson, Henry J.	L			Rallings, Peter J.	I	
Pflaum, Andrew	C			Ranier, William C.	D	
Pfund, Sebastian	D			Ranson, Henry P.	A	
Pfund, Sebastian	D			Rarey, George	E	
Phifer, John F.	G			Raspen, John	A	
Phillips, Edmondson	D			Rautenberg, William J.	H	
Phillips, Homer C.	F			Rawley, John	C	
Phillips, Thomas H.	M			Ray, Henry	D	
Phillipson, Samuel	M			Rea, Edward	K	
Philpot, Frank H.	B			Rea, John W.	K	
Pickett, James L.	E			Rea, Runkle	L	
Pilney, Charles G.	K			Reed, Bayler F.	F	
Pipes, Ashel E.	M			Reese, Bayliss T.	F	
Piterion, Alex W.	G			Reid, August	I	
Pitger, William F.	E			Reilly, Bernard J.	B	
Pittman, David C.	K			Reily, John	K	
Pitts, Charles	K			Reinalds, John W.	A	
Pitts, William C.	B			Reinberg, Ferdinand	M	
Pond, George	A			Rekucky, Joseph	M	
Ponlin, John W.	C			Remer, Edgar L.	I	
Portman, Charles E.	M			Rendler, William H.	M	

Respp, Mather	H	Ruhl, Jacob	H
Reynolds, B.	M	Ruhlenbeck, Louis H.	A
Reynolds, Eliot D.	A	Ruilligan, James	K
Reynolds, Henry	A	Rundes, Floyd H.	B
Reynolds, John T.	I	Rusch, Paul E.	C
Reynolds, Lyman	D	Ruse, Volney	L
Reynolds, Melan	M	Russell, John C.	J
Reynolds, Yeatman P.	M	Russon, Alfonso	M
Rhodes, Thomas D.	M	Ryan, Arther	I
Rich, Harry	K	Ryan, George C.	H
Rich, James	K	Ryan, John D.	C
Richards, Edward	E	Rycavy, Venel	K
Ricker, John F.	E	Rylander, Carl O.	E
Ricot, John	B	Rysdale, Peter	E
Rigan, Willam P.	F	Rystedt, Magnus	K
Riley, Owen	A	Saab, Abraham	M
Rinkel, Albert W.	C	Sackett, George F.	H
Roach, Douglas	L	Sackett, George T.	
Roark, John R.	I	Sahs, Edward H.	M
Robbins, Morris	B	Salisbury, Alfonso, A.	B
Roberts, Charles E.	D	Salwitihka, Joseph	E
Roberts, Clifford S.	D	Salwitzki, Joseph	E
Roberts, John	B	Sambuch, James F.	B
Roberts, Revez A.	H	Samuel, Nathan	D
Robinson, Frederick	E	Sanborn, Herbert W.	H
Robinson, Henry J.	L	Sandberg, Oscar F.	C
Roblyn, Raymond C.	M	Sanders, Leslie	E
Roche, John J.	F	Sanders, William M.	L
Roff, John L.	B	Sandewey, Richard	B
Rogers, Joseph C.	C	Sandford, Joseph A.	E
Rogers, Joseph H.	D	Sandwig, Frederich	I
Roobsby, George	F	Sarsh, Henry	M
Rose, Leslie H.	K	Sawyer, Charles	F
Rosengreen, Noah	E	Scarborough, William E.	B
Rosin, Benjamin	M	Schaefer, Otto	L
Rosin, Fred W.	G	Schafer, August	E
Rosin, Robert R.	M	Schaffer, Frederick	G
Roskowinski, Joseph	K	Schaiffer, Charles J.	F
Ross, Albert W.	B	Scharff, Henry	H
Ross, Wirt L.	C	Schenk, John E.	G
Rubeck, Albert	G	Schenk, William G.	M
Rubley, Evan	H	Schmidt, Frank	D
Ruger, Albert	L	Schmidt, Geoffrey	F

Schmith, George	K		Shebord, John	M
Schmitt, Charles	M		Sheehan, Cornelius	K
Schneider, Charles F.	G		Shehan, James	K
Scholl, William P.	B		Sheldon, Robert	B
Schontz, John H.	C		Shellhardt, Herman	K
Schrach, Charles F.	C		Shelton, William E.	G
Schrader, Carl	C		Shenk, Alvin	B
Schreiber, George	L		Shepard, Howard	A
Schrock, Paul E.R.	K		Shepperd, William	K
Schroeder, Theodor	E		Sherer, Homer J.	E
Schuler, Herman	A		Sherman, George	L
Schuler, Joseph	B		Shields, William N.	F
Schulgr, Paul	K		Shine, Edward W.	F
Schultz, Arthur	B		Shively, Frederick	C
Schultze, John W.	L		Shofield, Charles B.	A
Schurstedh, Ferdinand	M		Sickert, William H.	F
Schuyler, Rutson V.	K		Sidenberger, Frederick	B
Schwenk, John E.	G		Siehl, Fred	K
Scomalski, Frank	A		Sikers, Harry	B
Scott, Boyd	M		Silcox, Smith	M
Scott, Clinton C.	E		Silsby, Archie M.	E
Sculley, William J.	B		Silverbrand, Claude	D
Searle, Charles	L		Simcorski, Frank	M
Sebald, Max	E		Simmons, James W.	M
Sechard, Elmar	L		Simpkins, Clarence E.	K
Seher, Henry A.	B		Sinton, Benjamin	G
Sehr, Oscar S.	H		Siran, Lewis	L
Sell, Jacob H.	I		Siskind, Morris	G
Sgrwegk, Joachim	A		Sivartz, Christ	A
Shaber, Rudolph	M		Siwert, Emil	B
Shackler, Charles A.	M		Skirsa, Stanislaus	M
Shadon, Albert L.	F		Skogland, Oscar	E
Shallitz, William	F		Slack, Joseph	M
Shank, Victor C.	B		Slade, John H.	D
Sharp, Felix C.	G		Slankard, William H.	K
Sharp, Henry	H		Sleter, John	K
Sharp, John W.	M		Sletteland, Chris	C
Shater, Joseph W.	D		Smarten, Christ.	A
Shatus, Michael	K		Smith, Arthur	C
Shaw, John D.	M		Smith, Edward J.	M
Shea, Michael	C		Smith, Frank O.	M
Shea, William	L		Smith, George L.	B
Shea, Joseph W.	B		Smith, Henry	A

Smith, Mack	F		Strand, Jery T.	L
Smith, Samuel	I		Strand, Thomas L.	L
Smith, Stanley M.	I		Strant, Walter H.	K
Smith, William V.	D		Stratton, Kendall A.	L
Smith, William W.	B		Strong, Clinton S.	C
Snidow, James H.	L		Styx, Andrew	A
Snyder, Edwin B.	C		Subber, Anthony O.	L
Sodeman, August	M		Suhrs, Robert J.	K
Sollman, August A.	E		Sullivan, Patrick J.	C
Spangler, George W.	K		Sullivan, Timothy	C
Stacy, Henry	I		Summers, William H.	K
Stahl, Paul E.	B		Suok, Thomas W.	A
Stammach, John M.	E		Surber, Charles E.	G
Standafed, Charles	D		Surnsen, Albert	C
Stanfield, Jerry E.	H		Sutton, Robert	L
Stangel, Ferdinand	E		Swanson, Adolph	B
Stanhope, Nelson B.	M		Swanson, Charles E.	M
Starace, Charles	K		Sweet, Joseph D.	M
Stark, George	M		Swigh, William J.	D
Stauffer, Arthur C.	A		S???, Frank S.[235]	G
Steagall, James	L		Syphers, Ralph J.	G
Stenger, Clarence G.	B		Szepan, Michael	C
Steven, August F.	L		Szymonajkys, John	A
Stevens, Thomas M.	B		Tabor, Samuel	B
Stevenson, Edgar J.	M		Tade, Charles F.	D
Steward, James S.	K		Tanner, Edward J.	G
Steyer, Chauncey G.	F		Tanser, Georg N.	M
Stifler, Charles H.	H		Tausau, George K.	M
Stigers, Harry J.	G		Taylor, Charles E.	I
Stigs, Harry J.	G		Taylor, William	A
Stiles, Elba	M		Taylor, William R.	L
Stine, Edward U.			Thatch, Walter A.	I
Stine, Edwin C.	H		Thatcher, Grank	E
Stokes, Charles	E		Thayer, Albert W.	G
Stokes, Edward J.	D		Thiesson, Harry J	D
Stokes, Frank J.	G		Thomas, Anton	M
Stone, L.	A		Thomas, Arthur	M
Stone, William	D		Thomas, Arthur C.	M
Stonge, Albert B.	M		Thomas, Benjamin J.	K
Storms, Mason W.	K		Thomas, Daniel	L
Storr, Roy	L		Thomas, David J.	
Stouck, Maurter J.	G			
Stragland, Oscar	E			

---

[235] **Name cannot be determined.**

Thomas, Henry R.	F	Vandergrift, Charles F.	H
Thompson, Francis	K	Vanderslice, William	G
Thompson, Frederick	A	Vesaey, Samuel	K
Thompson, Henry A.	F	Vinger, Grapen A.	G
Thompson, Thomas H.	D	Vogel, Henry G.E.	K
Thompson, William	M	Voget, Henry G.E.	K
Thompson, William H.	M	Vogler, Ricahrd	C
Tilghman, Lionel B.	M	Voth, Herman F.	K
Tisthammer, Bert. B.	D	Wadd, Charlie	H
Toland, Andrew	L	Wagner, Charles E.	K
Tolbart, William R.	K	Wagner, Otto	I
Tolbert, John A.	K	Waite, Edard	F
Tollefson/Tolefson, Benjamin A.	B	Waldroop, John R.	M
Tollert, Michael J.	I	Walker, James O.	M
Tombly, Alexander	G	Walker, John D.	F
Tompkins, George A.	F	Wallan, William	A
Tompkins, Walter T.	I	Walline, Frank O.S.	B
Toohey, Dennis	D	Walser, Richard	G
Toohey, James	D	Walsh, James P.	L
Took, Mickel	E	Walstrom, Emil	H
Townbly, Alexander	G	Ward, William, Jr.	K
Townsend, Arley	F	Ware, John C.	F
Tracey, John	H	Wash, Absalom	L
Tranz, George	K	Waters, John F.	G
Truckenbront, George	M	Watson, Edward	K
Truitt, Albert	D	Watson, Frank C.	E
Truman, Marion F.	C	Weat, Henry J	G
Trump, Fred D.	L	Webb, James H.	K
Tucker, William	D	Weber, Edwin H.	E
Tucker, William	E	Weber, Edwin H.	E
Turner, Robert F.	C	Webster, James A.	H
Turrp, John H.	K	Weibel, Shando	A
Tustin, Charles	C	Weis, August	H
Tyler, Frederick G.	M	Welhansen, Fred	I
Underwood, Thomas T.	M	Welsh, Edward L.	K
Ure, Herbert	K	Wengel, Leonard	H
Utt, Harry I.	I	Werd, Charles	B
Vail, Arthur	D	Wesolowski, Frank	M
Vail, Charles S.	D	West, Fred	I
Vallancourt, Oliver	I	Westerhold, Charles	L
Van Kirk, Ira H.	L	Westfall, John W.	K
Vander Ake, Charles A.	K	Wheeler, Leroy A.	E
		White, Colin	B

Name		Name	
White, George W.	G	Wirpel, Frank	D
White, Joseph	F	Witt, Boyd	M
White, Louis R.	F	Wittiche, Robert S.	G
White, Oscar	K	Wolfe, Walter E.	M
White, William B.	L	Woliver, Silas	C
Whiteningsly, Henry	B	Wood, Harry E.	K
Whitesell, Fred	B	Wood, Isaac H.	L
Whitlock, Guy L.	M	Wood, John H.	K
Whitman, Joseph M.	B	Wood, Patrick J.	M
Whitsell, Fred	B	Wood, Robert C.	D
Whittaker, Simon	M	Woodard, Fred D.	B
Wianns, Andrew M.	K	Woodside, John T.	F
Wicks, William	H	Woodward, Fred D.	B
Wiedoff, Ernst	I	Woodwill, Henry	A
Wilde, Walter	L	Wooley, Guy	C
Wilhelm, Jonnie	A	Wooshell, Archibald A.	E
Wilkins, Harry O.	C	Worchenross, Victor	G
Will, Frank	H	Worm, John W.	K
Willard, Charles D.	G	Worrick, Clay D.	E
Willi, Otto	C	Worworth, Robert	M
Williams, Charles	L	Wright, John	C
Williams, James S.	M	Wrnzre, Leaman	H
Williams, John	D	Wunistz, Frank	D
Williams, Thomas J.	D	Wunner, Fred	K
Wilson, Albert	G	Yates, George S.	M
Wilson, John	B	Yeager, George	K
Wilson, Joseph W.	G	Yetman, Aubran	E
Wilson, Marshell	M	Young, Frank F.	C
Wilson, Roy C.	F	Zaccarice, Zascasilla	D
Winder, Fred C.	K	Zeigler, John G.	F
Winfrey, Joseph C.	L	Zimmerman, Emanual H.	D
Winkler, Hugh M.	G		
Winkler, Josef/Joseph H.	F		

Combat Casualty List

Name	Rank	Co	Nature of Casualty
Battle near Caloocan (25 March 1899)			
Ingahm, John	Private	G	Killed in Action
Nelson, Nels	Private	G	Killed in Action
Cummings, Marten	Corporal	M	Killed in Action
Norris, Thomas P.	Private	M	Killed in Action
Merrill, Willard J.	Private	M	Killed in Action
Hamilton, Jack	Private	E	shot in right thigh
O'Malley, Michael	Private	E	shot in left forearm
Owens, George	Private	F	shot in right leg
Heberling, William H.	Corporal	G	shot through stomach; died 31 March 1899
Fitzgerald, William H.	Corporal	M	shot left arm
Karger, Charles	Private	M	shot left shoulder
Warmworth, Robert H.	Private	M	unknown
Schenk, William G.	Private	M	unknown
Buchen, Frank	Private	M	unknown
Fenton, Charles M.	Private	M	unknown
Slack, Joseph	Private	M	shot left arm
Reinberg, Ferdinand	Private	M	unknown
McCullough, John L.	Private	M	shot left arm
Parrott, John W.	Private	M	shot left torso
Steigers, H.J.	Private	G	Missing In Action
Battle of Malolos (31 March 1899)			
Kissler, Robert C.	Private	B	shot in right forearm
Krohn, Emil	Private	A	shot in groin
Humphrey, Chauncey B.	2nd Lt	H	shot in left forearm
Horn, Ernest V	Corporal	H	flesh wound; calf, left leg

DeHart, Charles B.	Private	M	shot forehead
Battle of San Roque (29 April 1899)			
Todd, Charles C	2nd Lt		severely wounded in groin
Bevan, Oscar	Private	L	slight wound, right arm and side
Rea, Edward	Private	K	slight wound, right leg
Battle of San Miquel (23 May 1899)			
Whitlow, Guy L.	Private	M	Killed in Action
Pipes, Aksel P.	Corporal	M	Mortally wounded in action; died that evening.
McArthur, John C.	1st Lt	M	wounded, right leg; severely
Baker, Fred A.	Private	F	wounded, spine; severely
Wilson, John E.	Private	K	wounded, left thigh; severely
Frank, Richard T.	Private	C	wounded, in neck; slight
Baker, James H.	Private	K	wounded, right thigh; slight
Bowyer, Anthony	Private	A	wounded, left foot; severely
Higgings, Peter	Private	H	wounded, left foot; Slight
LeMay, William		F	wounded, right leg; slight
Miller, Joseph W.	Sergeant	H	wounded, right shoulder; severely
Percell, David J.	Private	K	wounded, right side; severely
Alpren, Samuel	Private	F	wounded, left leg; slight
Legenwood, Benjamin	Private	H	wounded, left foot; slight
Hellriegel, Jacob	Sergeant	K	wounded, left side; severely
Dietrick, Charles	Private	A	wounded, left arm; slight
Battle near Baliuag (26 May 899)			
Gamble, Charles	Private	C	wounded in head; died 11 June 1899
Anderson, Stanley	Private	C	wounded in groin, slight

Battle near Guingua (Bintong Church) (13/14 August 1899)				
Foster, William	Private	B	gunshot wound, right leg from Mauser; severely
Brooks, Charles A.	Private	F	Killed in Action
Jackson, Max	Private	C	drowned
Larson, Peters	Corporal	G	drowned
Actions near San Ildefenso (24 Nov 1899)			
Keyes, Maxwell	2nd Lt	L	Killed in Action; shot through head
Stone, L.	Private	A	flesh wound right thigh
Action Near Apalit (3 April 1900)			
Sheehan, Cornelius	QM Sgt	K	Left Manila 3 April 1900 in banca for Apalit, PI and never heard of since. Dropped June 15, 1900 as having been killed by ladrones. Authority for dropping contained in endorsement of Department Commander on approved finding of a Board of Officers.
Deaver, George	Sergeant	K	
Hansen, Christ E.	Private	K	
Battle of Tibaguin (3 July 1900)			
Merriam, Alfred W.	Sergeant	H	Killed in Action
Cheatham, William	Private	H	Killed in Action
Gaddy, Charles	Private	H	Mortally Wounded in Action
Burdt, Herman F.	Private	H	gunshot wounds in right arm, right hand and left arm; serious
Wade, Charles	Private	H	gunshot wound in right elbow; serious
Battle on Santa Cruz River (4 July 1900)			
Gocke, Albert	Corporal	G	Killed in Action; shot through the heart. Died

				instantaneous.
Muller, Patrick	Private	G		Mortally wounded in action; shot in forehead
Hippler, Charles L.	Private	G		Mortally wounded in action; shot through abdomen
Action at Near Guiguinto (16 September 1900)				
Helmcke, Max G.C.	Private	G		gunshot wounds in right hand/ right arm; powder burns in face/eyes; not serious
Lamon, Isaac J.	Private	G		gunshot wounded in left hand; not serious
Action on Caluate River (24 November 1900)				
Winkler, Josef H.	Private	F		Killed in Action; shot through neck; died of hemorrhage immediately
Harkins, Daniel O.	Private	L		Wounded in action; shot through face and neck
Kruger, Otto	Private	L		Wounded in action; shot through head
Miscellaneous Events				
Scheu, Otto	Corporal	B		POW/MIA- "supposed to have been captured and killed by bandits, July 21, 1899"; near Guingua; returned by insurgents on 24 October.
Fiedler, Cristof A.	Corporal	A		KIA; 29 Sept 1900 at Malolos; Missing; supposed to have been killed or captured by insurgents while on duty as Provost Corporal in Malolos.
Stigers, Harry J.	Private	G		MIA; Missing in action on 25 March 1899; rejoined company on 1 April 1899

Wallace, Frank	Corporal	H	MEDAL OF HONOR RECOMMENDATION- Downgraded to a CERTIFICATE OF MERIT- In the affair of July 2nd at Tibaguin, Corporal Frank Wallace, Company H, specially distinguished himself by promptly taking command as soon as Sergeant Merriam was killed, and with his detachment gallantly charging and driving back a force of armed natives, four or five times greater in number than his own party. (344747 A.G.O.)
Calkins, Charles	Private	E	Died of Wounds

Losses in combat operations include 16 killed in action, seven mortally wounded in action (23 total combat deaths), two drowned during combat operations (non-hostile deaths) and 43 men were wounded in action for 68 total combat losses. One Private, Robert McNave was WIA the night of 22 October 1899 when 25 insurgents attacked his company's outpost but the wound was reported as the result of one of his own rounds exploding in his cartridge belt.

Two men were missing in action. Harry J. Stigers, Co. G was missing for six days in late March 1899 and Otto Scheu, Co. B was a POW from about 21 July 1899 until released by insurgents on 24 October 1899. Four men were reported as 'deserters' and ended up becoming Filipino prisoners. These included Otto Wagner, Albert Rubeck, Peter J. Rallings and Archie Gordon. Reported absent on 11 October 1899, Gordon was returned to U.S. forces on 28 January 1900. The others, deserting around 28 July 1899, were returned in the prisoner exchange that included Scheu on 24 October.

Non-Hostile Deaths and Events

The three year period reflects nearly 80 non-combat deaths: five suicides, eight deaths by accident, one death by a domestic fight, over 60 deaths by disease. Approximately 50 men deserted. The ranks of all personnel are 'Private' unless otherwise noted. 'Disease' means 'Died of Disease'

Name	Co	Notes
Adams, Allen P.	E	Disease; malaria fever
Anderson, Fred	C	Disease; 24 Aug 99
Baker, George H.	E	Deserted; 31 July in Manila; Deserted while absent sick; dropped 9 Sept 1899
Barker, Joseph	C	Disease; chronic dysentery; October 1900
Bauman, Edward	E	Disease; dysentery; March 1900
Baxter, Frank		Deserted before departure
Begley, John	K	Accidentally shot and killed at target position (Note: training accident?); December 1900
Betterton, Philip G.	A	Deserted; Corporal; A; 20 August 1899 at Baliuag
Bobo, Benjamin E.	A	Deserted 15 Feb 1902; Malabon
Booth, John W.	G	Deserted 21 March 1901 at Guiguinto; Dropped 5 March 1901
Byrd, James W.	C	Disease; typhus; June 1901
Cadle, Jeff	G	Disease; malarial fever; June 1901
Cameron, James R.	E	Disease; 19 Oct 1899; Tetanus
Campbell, John	I	Accidentally drowned in Bag Bag River near Hagonoy; 11 Oct 1901
Carroll, Richard	B	Disease; 21 April 1899
Carter, Robert N.	F	Disease; 26 April 1899
Carter, Robert N.	F	Disease; 26 April 1899
Cauble, Thomas O.	D	Disease; 21 April 1899
Clifford, John	H	Deserted 11 Dec 1900 at Hagonoy.
Cogan, John H.	F	Disease; suspected smallpox; January 1900

Cook, Frank H.	D	Deserted 9 Sept 1901 at Malabon; Dropped 19 Sept 1899; Apprehended San Fernando, 29 Sept 1901
Crawford, Harry C.	D	Deserted 26 May 1900 at San Fernando; Dropped 5 June 1900.
Crego, Oscar	L	Deserted before departure
Daniby, Michael	E	Suicide; 5 Dec 1901
Davis, Hugh L.	L	Deserted 16 Feb 1901 at Malolos.
Devlin, George	M	Disease; at sea on ATS *Sherman*
Dries, Theodore	K	Deserted before departure
Dunbar, Roy S.	G	Deserted 17 Feb 1901 at Guiguinto; Dropped 1 March 1901
Duncan, Charles E.	B	Accidentally killed by Manila & Dagupan Railroad train near Bocar, PI; 18 August 1901
Dunlap, Harry G.	G	Deserted 27 July 1899 at Baliuag; Dropped 6 Aug 99; apparently killed by insurgents as his body was reported Gen. Grant as found and disinterred on 8 February 1900.
Dunn, John L.		Deserted before departure
Dunnaway, William	C	Disease; 30 Oct 1899; chronic diarrhea
Earnshaw, Albert	B	Deserted 17 Feb 1900 at Malabon.
Edwards, William	D	Deserted 3 Sept 1901 at Malabon; Dropped 13 Sept 1901.
Elder, Alvin E.	G	Disease; 7 Aug 99; Corporal
Esterly, Jacob R.	I	Deserted 2 Jan 1901 at Calumpit; Dropped 13 Jan 1901; Returned to duty 15 Jan 1901; Manila
Foster, William	A	Accidentally drowned; March 1900
Frank, Richard T.	C	Disease; fever and dysentery; February 1900
Gardner, James G.	B	Disease; March 1900; Corporal
Glazier, Leo J.	B	Deserted 7 Aug 1899 at Guingua.

Gordon, Archie	K	Listed as deserted 11 Oct 99 in Quingua; captured; Returned 28 January 1900; "surrendered by Insurgents authorities Jan 28, 1900"
Gragert, John	K	Disease; dysentery
Gray, James	H	Died of Wounds; from gunshot received in a fight near Company quarters with another soldiers
Grimes, Lundy Lee	C	Disease; pulmonary tuberculosis; October 1900; Corporal
Harney, John F.	L	Deserted 4 Sept 1901 in Manila; Surrendered on board USAT THOMAS off Kobe, Japan, 13 Sept 1901; dropped from rolls 17 Sept 1901; discharged by sentence of General Court Martial, 29 Jan 1902, S.O. 21, Dept of California 1902
Harrison, William E.	K	Disease; dysentery while en route U.S.; January 1902
Haskell, Frank	L	Deserted 7 Dec 1901; While on detached service
Haworth, Benjamin F.	C	Disease; Dysentery; January 1900
Helun, Palmer	H	Disease; 30 Aug 99
Hempstead, Arthur	F	Disease; Typhoid fever, 5 Oct 1901
Heston, Ernest C.	B.	Deserted 20 March 1900 at Malabon; Dropped as deserter 20 Mar 99.
Hochley, Edward W.	L	Disease; malarial fever; May 1901
Hodges, John W.	B	Deserted 19 July 1901 at Caloocan; Apprehended at Manila, 10 August 1901; discharged by General Court Martial (GCM), 4 Oct 1901 per Special Order (S.O.) 257, Dept of Northern Luzon, 29 Sept 1901
Hunt, Arthur L.	K	Disease; 8 May 1899
Hurst, Arthur S.	K	Disease; 8 May 1899

Hutchins, Lewis J.	L	Deserted 22 Aug 1899 in Manila while absent sick; dropped 16 Sept 1899.
Johnson, Martin	D	Disease; 22 Sept 1899; dysentery
Jones, William T.	E	Deserted 15 July 1900 at Meycauayan; Dropped 26 July 1900.
Jordan, John	K	Disease; Chronic diarrhea; August 1900
Karger, Charles	M	Disease; 29 May 1899
Kehoe, James	B	Accident; Killed by engine on Manila and Dagupan Railroad; not in the line of duty; 8 September 1901
Keller, William J.	F	Disease; malarial fever; June 1900
Kelsh, William D.	C	Accidentally drowned in Rio Grande River
Kent, William S.	K	Disease; acute dysentery; Aug 1900
Kirwan		Deserted before departure
Knapp, Russell S.	BAND	Disease; Dysentery; July 1900
Krueger, Fred	K	Disease; July 1899
Kuhlsubach, Louis H.	A	Deserted 15 Feb 1901 at Malabon.
Larson, Louis	M	Deserted 31 Jan 1900 at Bulacan.
Larson, Peter	G	Disease; 14 Aug 99; Corporal
Leasch, Arthur J.	M	Disease; chronic dysentery; September 1900
Lehman, Henry	M	Accident; Died of Wounds; 5 May 1899; accidental shooting near Maasin
MacArthur, George	B	Sergeant; Deserted 16 Jan 1902 at Caloocan; Dropped as deserter 20 Jan 1902
Matter, Edward N.	BAND	Disease; 11 March 1899/died of disease in the hospital of the transport *Sherman* of pernicious malarial fever
Mauz, Peter	F	Disease; July 1899

McCarthy, Felix	L		Deserted 14 Nov 1901 at Malolos; Dropped 25 Nov 1901.
McDonough, Bernard	F		Disease; Chronic diarrhea; March 1900
McGuire, Thomas J.	D		Suicide; self-inflicted gunshot wound; December 1900
McKnight, James			Deserted before departure
Meehan, Hugh F.	H		Deserted 14 Jan 1901 in Hagonoy; Dropped 24 Jan 1901.
Mennon, John	C		Disease; 17 August 1899
Metzger, William R.	B		Disease; typhoid fever; May 1901
Mitchell, Alexander	H		Deserted 11 July 1899 in Manila while absent sick.
Mounty, William B.	L		Deserted 30 April 1899 at Apalit while in camp.
Nieman, George	E		Disease; Phthisis; May 1901
Palmer, Frank A.	L		Deserted 25 June 1899 while in confinement
Parcell, David J.	K		Disease; Chronic dysentery; December 1900
Parker, Charles E.	K		Deserted 2 Oct 1900 in Apalit; Dropped as deserter 12 Oct 1900; Apprehended at Manila, 23 Nov 1900; rejoined Company 25 Nov 1900; discharged by GCM 8 Feb 1901, Apalit, S.O. 16, Dept of Northern Luzon, 17 Jan 1901.
Parker, Patrick J.	G		Disease; 14 Feb 1901; of abscess of the liver; noted in March muster.
Patterson, Joseph C.	L		Disease; malarial fever; June 1900
Patton, Frank A.	K		Suicide, self inflicted gunshot wounds.
Peachhouse, Squire	L		Deserted 31 Dec 1899 n Honolulu while en route to join unit from US.
Pfund, Sebastian	D		Suicide by hanging; 25 Sept 1901
Rallings, Peter J.	I		Deserted 28 July 1899 at Baliuag; Dropped 8 Aug 99; captured by insurgents; " Deserted July 28. Apprehended October 28, 1899."

Reese, Bayliss T.	F	Disease; smallpox
Rich, Harry	K	Disease; chronic dysentery; 17 November 1900
Romanovizc, Ignacy	D	Disease; 18 Nov 1899; dysentery
Roskowinski, Joseph	K	Died; Pulmonary tuberculosis; March 1902
Rubeck, Albert	G	Deserted 8 Sept 1899 at Baliuag; Dropped 17 Sept 99; captured by insurgents; "Deserter July 26. Apprehended October 27, 1899"
Sackett, George F	H	Deserted 26 July 1899 at Baliuag; Dropped 6 Aug 99; Apprehended at Victoria, PI on 8 Jan 1900.
Sackett, George F.	H	Deserter; recaptured
Salwitzki, Joseph	E	Disease; 22 May 1899
Sandford, Joseph A.	E	Deserted 16 July 1899 in San Fernando while on detached service.
Sawyer, Charles	F	Suicide, self inflicted gunshot wound to the head.
Schaffer, Frederick	G	Deserted before departure
Scharff, Henry	H	Disease; appendicitis; January 1901
Scholl, William P.	B	Disease; alcoholism; October 1900
Shater, Joseph W.	D	Deserted 3 July 1899 in Guingua; Dropped 10 Aug 1899
Shaw, John D.	M	Deserted 25 Sept 1901 in Bulacan; Dropped 4 October 1901; Corporal
Shea, Dennis J.	B	Deserted 30 Oct 1899 in Quingua.
Sivartz, Christ	A	Disease; 27 Sept 1899; Typhoid
Skogland, Oscar	E	Accidentally drowned near Bigaa, PI; 12 Jan 1902
Stacy, Henry	I	Deserted 28 July 1899 in Baliuag; Dropped 8 Aug 1899.
Storr, Roy	L	Disease; 26 Nov 1899; Typhoid

Name	Co.	Notes
Thomas, David J.	K?	Deserted while in camp on 30 April 1899; surrendered from desertion on 2 Jan 1902 in Louisville, Kentucky.
Tollefson/Tolefson, Benjamin A.	B	Disease; 23 Sept 1899; dysentery
Took, Mickel	E	Disease; Chronic Dysentery; May 1901
Tucker, William	D	Deserted 25 May 1900 in San Fernando; Dropped 5 June 1900
Vogt/Voget, Henry G.E.	K	Disease; Chronic diarrhea; August 1900
Wagner, Otto	I	Deserted 28 July 1899 in Baliuag; Dropped 8 Aug 99; Captured by insurgents; Deserted July 28. Apprehended Oct 28, 1899"
Walline, Frank O.S.	B	Disease; died while absent, sick on transport *Sheridan*; 8 Aug 1899
Weber, Edwin H.	E	Disease; 28 Aug 99
White, George W.	G	Disease; pulmonary tuberculosis; September 1900
Whitsell, Fred	B	Died 13 Jan 1901 en route US on transport *Sherman*; of chronic diarrhea (noted in March 1901 roll)
Wiedoff, Ernst	I	Disease; July 1899
Wightman, William	I	Disease; Multiple Neuritis; March 1900; Sergeant
Woodard, Fred D.	B	Disease; epileptic convulsions; Uly 1901
Worm, John W.	K	Disease; blood poisoning from insect bite; June 1900
Winze, Leaman	H	Disease; typhoid fever; January 1901

Bibliography

Primary Sources

American Imperialism and the Philippine Insurrection; Testimony taken from Hearings On Affairs in the Philippine Islands before the Senate Committee on the Philippines, 1902, edited by Henry Franklin Graff, Columbia University. Part of the 'Testimony of the Times: Selections from Congressional Hearings' Series, John A. Garraty, General Editor, Little, Brown & Company, Boston, 1969

Heitman, Francis B. Historical Register and Dictionary of the United States Army, From Its Organization, September 29, 1789, to March 2, 1903. (Washington: Government Printing Office), 1903.

Hix, John Franklin, personal interview, August 1976, by Greg Eanes; follow-on article published, *'Spanish-American War: 102-Year-Old Man Remembers It Well'*, The Crewe-Burkeville Journal, (August 26, 1976)

Pershing, John J., My Experiences In the First World War, De Capo Press, New York, 1995; originally published in 1931 by F.A. Stokes, New York

U.S. Congress
-*Affairs in the Philippine Islands: Hearings (April 10, 1902), Vol 3*. United States. Congress. Senate. Committee on the Philippines. (Washington, DC: GPO) 1902

-*Charges of Cruelty, etc., to the Natives of the Philippines: Letter from the Secretary of War Relative to the Reports and Charges in the Public Press of Cruelty and Oppression Exercised by Our Soldiers Toward Natives of the Philippines.* Document No. 205, Part 1, 57th Congress, Senate, 1st Session (Washington: GPO) 1902

- *"Chronological List of Actions with Losses from February 4, 1899 to June 30, 1899"*, Congressional Record, 56th Congress, 2nd Session, 1900, Microfilm Records, pages 858-870

- *"Chronological History of Military Operations",* Congressional Record, 56th Congress, 2nd Session, 1900, Microfilm Records, Appendix, pages 114-118

- *"History of Events",* Appendix, page 169, Congressional Record, 56th Congress, 1st Session, 1901, Microfilm Records

- *"Review of the Philippine Revolution By Aguinaldo",* Congressional Record, 57th Congress, 1st and Special, 1902, Microfilm Copy, Appendix, p.440

U.S. War Department
- *Annual Report of Major General Adna R. Chaffee, U.S. Army Commanding, Division of the Philippines, Military Governor of the Philippine Islands,* Vol. II, (1901). Period of report was from 1 August 1900 to 30 June 1901.

- *Annual Report of Major General Arthur MacArthur, U.S.V., Commanding, Division of the Philippines, Military Governor in the Philippine Islands,* Vol 1 and Vol 2 (1900). Covers the period from 5 May to 30 September 1900.

- *Annual Reports of the War Department for the Fiscal Year Ended June 30, 1900. Report of the Lieutenant-General Commanding the Army. In Seven Parts.* Part 5 and Part 6. (Washington: Government Printing Officer, 1900)

-*Annual Reports of the War Department for the Fiscal Year Ended June 30, 1902. Report of the Lieutenant-General Commanding the Army and Department Commanders .*Volume IX. (Washington: Government Printing Officer, 1902)

- *Correspondence of the Adjutant General's Office,* (AGO OR) Roll 564, Third Infantry Regiment, Index. (NARA Microcopy 698)

- *Correspondence Relating To The War With Spain and Conditions Growing Out of the Same, including the Insurrection In the Philippine Islands and the China Relief Expedition Between the*

Adjutant General of the Army and the Military Commanders in the United States, Cuba, Porto Rico, China, and the Philippine Islands from April 15, 1898 to July 30, 1902, with an appendix, in two Volumes, Volume 2, Government Printing Office, Washington, D.C., 1902

-*Five Years of the War Department Following the War with Spain, 1899-1903, as shown in the Annual Reports of the Secretary of War* (U.S. War Department) 1904

-*Official Army Register for 1899*. Adjutant General's Office (Washington) January 1, 1899

- *Philippine Insurgent Records*. Includes galley proofs of John R.M. Taylor's History of the Philippine Insurrection Against the United States, 1898-1903: A Compilation of Documents and Introduction, Washington, D.C., 1906 (NARA Microcopy 254)

-*Report of Major General E.S. Otis, U.S. Volunteers on Military Operations and Civil Affairs in the Philippine Islands.* (Washington: GPO) 1899. Period covered from 30 June 1898 to 31 August 1899.

-*Report of Major General E.S. Otis, U.S. Army, Commanding Division of the Philippines, Military Governor, September 1, 1899 to May 5, 1900..* (Washington: GPO) 1900.

- *Report of Brigadier General F.D. Grant, U.S. Volunteers, of operations of Second Brigade, Second Division, Eighth Army Corps, from November 1, 1899 to April 15, 1900;* Annual Reports of War Department for Fiscal Year Ended June 30, 1900; Part 5, p65

-*Report of Brigadier General F.D. Grant, HDQRS, Commanding Fifth District, Department of Northern Luzon, April 15, 1901 to Adjutant General;* Narrative report of military operations; Annual Reports of the War Department for the Fiscal Year Ended June 30, 1901, Part 3; p135

- *Returns from Regular Army Infantry Regiments*, June 1821-December 1916, Roll 37, Third Infantry Regiment, January 1895 to December 1899 (NARA Microcopy 665)

- *Returns from Regular Army Infantry Regiments*, June 1821-December 1916, Roll 38, Third Infantry Regiment, January 1900 to December 1905. (NARA Microcopy 665)

Williams, Ora. Oriental American: Official and Authentic Records of the Dealings of the United States with the Natives of Luzon and their Former Rulers (Oriental American Publishing Co: Chicago, 1899), p115-116

Secondary Sources
Books
Bain, David Haward, Sitting In Darkness: Americans in the Philippines, Boston, Penguin Books, Houghton Mifflin Company, 1986

Beede, Benjamin R., editor, The War of 1898 and U.S. Interventions 1898-1934: An Encyclopedia, New York & London, Garland Publishing Inc., 1994

Chant, Christopher, The Military History of the United States, Vol. 7, *'Border wars & Foreign Excursions'*, Marshall Cavendish, New York & London, 1992

Clodfelter, Michael, Warfare and Armed Conflicts: A Statistical Reference to Casualty and Other Figures, 1618-1991, Vol. II, 1900-1901. Jefferson, NC: McFarland & Company, Inc., 2002

Collins, John M., America's Small Wars: Lessons For The Future, Brassey's (US) Inc., A MacMillian Publishing Company, 8000 Westpark Drive, McLean, Va 22102, 1991

Joes, Anthony James, Guerilla Warfare: A Historical, Biographical, and Bibliographical Sourcebook, Westport, CT, Greenwood Press, Greenwood Publishing Company, 1996

Linn, Brian McAllister, The Philippine War 1899-1902, Lawrence, Kansas, University of Kansas Press, 2000

Linn, Brian McAllister, The U.S. Army And Counterinsurgency in the Philippine War, 1899-1902, Chapel Hill, The University of North Carolina Press, 1989

Maring, Ester G., Historical and Cultural Dictionary of the Philippines, Washington, Series Three in Historical and Cultural Dictionaries of Asia, 1973

Matloff, Maurice, American Military History, Vol. 1, 1775-1902, Combined Books, Conshohocken, Pa, 1996

Special Operations Research Office, A Summary of the U.S. Role in Insurgency Situations in the Philippine Islands, 1899-1955, Special Operations Research Office, The American University, 1964, Washington, D.C.

Wolf, Leon, Little Brown Brother: How the U.S. Purchased and Pacified the Philippine Islands At the Century's Turn, Doubleday and Co., Inc., Garden City, New York, 1961

Magazine Articles

Filiberti, Edward J., 'The *Roots of U.S. Counterinsurgency Doctrine'*, Military Review, January 1988, p. 50-61

Ganley, Eugene F., *'Springfields and Bolos'*, Military Review, July 1961, Vol. XLI, No. 7, p. 47-54

Kohler, David R., and James W. Wensyel, 'Our *First Southeast Asian War'*, American History Illustrated, January-February, 1990, Vol. 24, p. 18-31

May, Glenn A., A Review of the 'Battle *for Batangas: A Philippine Province At War'*, Small Wars and Insurgencies, Vol. 2, No. 2, August 1991, Frank Cass & Company Ltd, London

About the Author

Colonel Greg Eanes retired from the Air Force in August 2011 after more than 34 years service (to include eight years Navy enlisted time). He has multiple wartime and expeditionary deployments. The author of several regional military histories, he is a native of Nottoway County, Virginia and the former General Manager of The Crewe-Burkeville Journal. He is a former advanced placement history teacher for Charlotte County (Va) Public Schools and adjunct to Southside Virginia Community College. Prior to 9/11 activation, he was an adjunct lecturer on Community Leadership at the Wilson Center for Leadership in the Public Interest at Hampden-Sydney College. He served on the faculty of the Air Force Intelligence School as the lead instructor for Special Operations/Low Intensity Conflict (SO/LIC) studies and was on the adjunct faculty at the Joint Military Intelligence Training Center (JMITC) at the Defense Intelligence Agency (DIA). He holds a Master's Degree in Military History from American Military University and Bachelor's Degree in Occupational Education (now Workforce Education and Development) from Southern Illinois University-Carbondale. He is a graduate of the Air War College and Air Command and Staff College. Married to the former Rosanne Lukoskie of Shamokin, Pennsylvania, they have two adult daughters and a son-in-law now serving in the U.S. Marine Corps.

www.ingramcontent.com/pod-product-compliance
Lightning Source LLC
Chambersburg PA
CBHW061653040426
42446CB00010B/1714